W9-BWC-741

LIBERIA
in Pictures

Thomas Streissguth

TF
CB
Twenty-First Century Books

Contents

Lerner Publishing Group realizes that current information and statistics quickly become out of date. To extend the usefulness of the Visual Geography Series, we developed www.vgsbooks.com, a website offering links to up-to-date information, as well as in-depth material, on a wide variety of subjects. All of the websites listed on www.vgsbooks.com have been carefully selected by researchers at Lerner Publishing Group. However, Lerner Publishing Group is not responsible for the accuracy or suitability of the material on any website other than www.lernerbooks.com. It is recommended that students using the Internet be supervised by a parent or teacher. Links on www.vgsbooks.com will be regularly reviewed and updated as needed.

Twenty-First Century Books
A division of Lerner Publishing Group
241 First Avenue North
Minneapolis, MN 55401 U.S.A.

Website address: www.lernerbooks.co

web enhanced @ www.vgsbooks.com

Library of Congress Cataloging-in-Publication Data

Streissguth, Thomas, 1958–
    Liberia in pictures / by Tom Streissguth.
      p. cm. — (Visual geography series)
    Includes bibliographical references and index.
    ISBN-13: 978-0-8225-2465-6 (lib. bdg. : alk. paper)
    ISBN-10: 0-8225-2465-1 (lib. bdg. : alk. paper)
    1. Liberia—Juvenile literature. 2. Liberia—Pictorial works—Juvenile literature. I. Title. II. Visual geography series (Minneapolis, Minn.)
DT624.S77 2006
966.62—dc22   2005004644

Manufactured in the United States of America
1 2 3 4 5 6 – BP – 11 10 09 08 07 06

INTRODUCTION

The western African nation of Liberia was established in 1847. Home to roughly 3.5 million people, the nation is Africa's oldest republic (country with an elected government). Yet it has suffered many years of ethnic conflict and civil war. By the twenty-first century, these troubles had turned Liberia into one of the world's poorest and most violent countries.

Long before it became a nation, Liberia was home to several dozen indigenous (native) groups, who lived in the region's tropical rain forests and coastal areas. In the early 1800s, freed slaves and the descendants of slaves from the United States settled in Liberia. In 1847 these Americo-Liberians declared their nation's independence and elected a president and a legislature (group of lawmakers). Although the Americo-Liberians made up just 5 percent of Liberia's population, they dominated the nation's government and economy.

Following Liberia's independence, countries around the world supported the new nation. Since it had been founded by freed slaves,

Liberia held out the promise of a new start and freedom for other people escaping slavery. Liberia's many natural resources, such as minerals and timber, attracted foreign investors. In the 1920s, the Firestone Tire and Rubber Company built a huge rubber-tree farm in Liberia. In the mid-twentieth century, Liberia enjoyed fast economic growth. Many people from the countryside poured into the cities to seek jobs and better homes.

In many ways, the move to cities increased the country's social divisions. The nation became both urban and rural, modern and traditional. In the rain forests of the interior, native people lived in small clearings, grew their own food, and elected clan chiefs to settle their disputes. In the cities, people of many ethnic backgrounds lived side by side and worked at various jobs. Political parties, representing different ethnic groups, vied for elected office and a majority in the legislature.

The mixture of groups created a vibrant cultural life in Liberia. But it also fueled long-standing feuds. Hostilities simmered for decades.

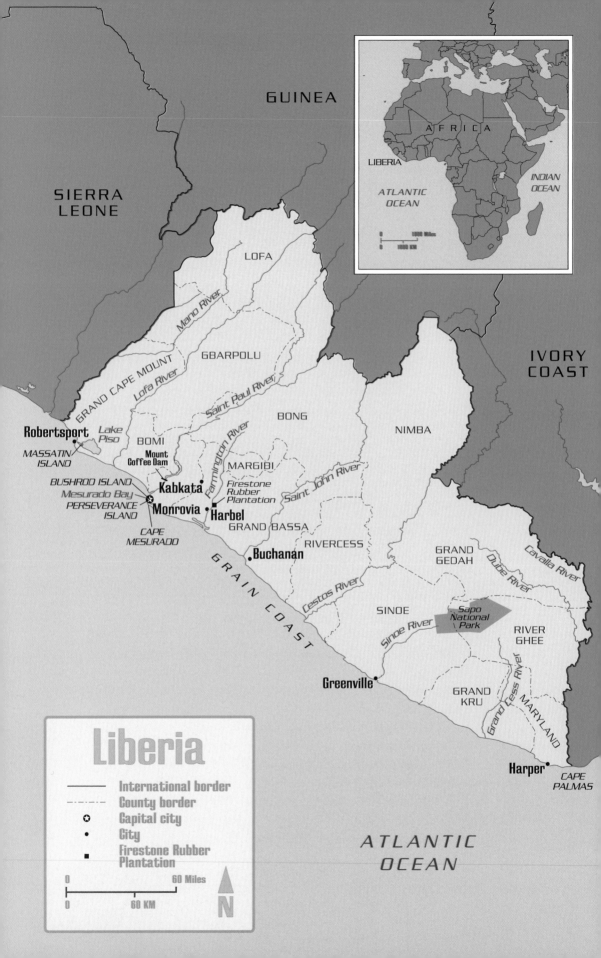

Then, in 1980, indigenous rebels overthrew the government. A civil war began in 1989. This war killed hundreds of thousands of people and destroyed the Liberian economy. Schools, hospitals, and businesses shut down. Liberians struggled just to find enough food and clean drinking water. Many Liberians fled the country to escape the violence and suffering.

In the mid-1990s, after a series of truces and peace agreements, the fighting began to die down. In 2003 the United Nations (UN)—an international peace and security organization—sent soldiers to keep order in Liberia and to disarm the rival political factions and their armies.

Liberia held its first free election in fourteen years in 2005, which led to a runoff between businesswoman and activist Ellen Johnson-Sirleaf and former Liberian soccer star George Manneh Weah. The media and some election officials declared Johnson-Sirleaf the winner in November, making her Liberia's—and Africa's—first democratically elected woman president. She vows to rebuild the country, unite the people, and bring an end to conflict. Weah and his supporters challenged the election result, claiming fraud.

Before the civil war, Liberia was seen as a success story among African nations. Despite the optimism of the 2005 election, it will likely take many years of hard work for Liberia to achieve that status again.

THE LAND

The Republic of Liberia is a small nation on the coast of western Africa. It lies just north of the equator, the imaginary line that divides the northern and southern halves of the earth. The Atlantic Ocean borders Liberia's long and low-lying seacoast. Sierra Leone neighbors Liberia to the northwest, while Guinea borders Liberia to the north. Côte D'Ivoire, or the Ivory Coast, forms Liberia's eastern border. The nation's total land area is 43,000 square miles (111,370 square kilometers). Liberia is slightly larger than either Tennessee or Ohio.

 Regions

Liberia is made up of three main geographical regions: coastal lowlands, inland plateaus (raised plains), and mountains. The coastal region measures 370 miles (595 km) long and about 50 miles (80 km) wide. The coastal lowlands are flat and fertile and include the nation's largest cities. Lagoons, marshes, and mangrove trees line the coast, and long sandbars lie just offshore.

Farther inland a band of plateaus runs across Liberia, reaching an average elevation of 1,000 feet (305 meters) above sea level. The plateaus gradually rise to steep hills in the north. Villages dot the plateau region, with many built along rivers that empty into the Atlantic Ocean. A dense rain forest, one of the largest rain forests in western Africa, covers the plateaus and hills.

Mountains are scattered around the nation. The Bong Range lies northeast of the Liberian capital of Monrovia, just 25 miles (40 kilometers) from the coast. In the northwest, the Mano Hills and the Wologizi Mountains rise between the Mano and Lofa rivers. Mount Wutivi in the Wologizi Mountains is Liberia's highest point. It reaches 4,613 feet (1,406 m) above sea level. The Nimba Mountains in the north are the site of iron ore mining operations. The Putu Range rises in southeastern Liberia, about 50 miles (80 km) northeast of the coastal town of Greenville.

Rivers and Lakes

The rivers of Liberia run northeast to southwest, following straight courses to the sea. The longest river, the Cavalla, forms the border between Liberia and the Ivory Coast. The second-longest river is the Saint Paul. It runs 125 miles (201 km) from the Nimba Mountains to Mesurado Bay at Monrovia. The Mano River forms part of Liberia's northwestern border with Sierra Leone. Other major rivers are the Saint John, the Lofa, the Cestos, and the Grand Cess.

During the rainy season, Liberia's roads turn to thick mud. So instead of using roads, people travel up and down rivers in shallow canoes. But canoeing on the rivers can be difficult. Sandbars, driftwood, and rocky river bottoms pose dangers to canoes. In addition to transportation, Liberians use rivers for irrigation, or watering crops. Before the civil war, hydroelectric power plants operated on the Saint Paul and several other Liberian rivers, but the plants were destroyed by the fighting.

The large, oblong Lake Piso covers about 40 square miles (103 sq. km) in Grand Cape Mount County in northwestern Liberia. The lake holds several small islands, including Massatin Island, named for a fifteenth-century woman who lived there. The island provided a refuge for people escaping the civil war of the 1990s.

> The name of Lake Piso stems from a native word meaning "pigeon's hole." Large flocks of pigeons used to fly to the lake to drink its waters.

Flora and Fauna

Tropical rain forests cover about 60 percent of the land in Liberia. The forest trees and plants are very valuable. For instance, rubber trees

A tapped rubber tree oozes latex into a pail. Liberian latex is prized for its use in making rubber goods.

provide latex, a substance used to make tires and other rubber products. People use teak, mahogany, walnut, and ironwood to build furniture. They use kola nuts to make medicines and soft drinks, liana vines to make footbridges, and palm trees to make thatch for roofing homes. Coffee plants, of course, provide coffee beans.

The Liberian rain forest also shelters a wide variety of animal life. The 3-foot-tall (1 m) pygmy hippopotamus thrives in Liberia and a few nearby nations. The country's rivers and riverbanks provide habitat for water buffalo, tortoises, crocodiles, and badgers. Several big cat species, including leopards, live in Liberia. The big cats prey on Liberia's plentiful monkeys, anteaters, antelopes, groundhogs, turtles, and honey badgers. Elephants live in Liberia too. The nation is also home to poisonous snakes, including cobras and pythons. The lagoons and marshes of Liberia's coastal areas attract birds such as spoonbills, egrets, and flamingos, while the forested interior hosts parrots, hawks, eagles, woodpeckers, and hornbills.

THE UNBELIEVABLE PYGMY HIPPO

Weighing 400 to 600 pounds (181 to 272 kilograms), the pygmy hippopotamus *(below)* is much smaller than the more common river hippopotamus, which can weigh up to 3,000 pounds (1,360 kg). Pygmy hippopotamuses have been found only in Liberia and a few nearby nations.

Scientists in Liberia first sighted the pygmy hippopotamus in 1849. They gave it the scientific name *Hexaprotodon liberiensis*. But for the next fifty-plus years, no scientist saw another pygmy hippopotamus. Many scientists thought the creature was extinct or that the person who made the original sighting had made a mistake. In reality, the shy pygmy hippo was simply staying well away from humans. Unlike ordinary hippos, the pygmy hippo does not spend much time in waterways, where people gather and travel.

In modern times, pygmy hippos live in zoos around the world. They also still live in western Africa, although their natural habitat (home) is under attack from mining, logging, and road building.

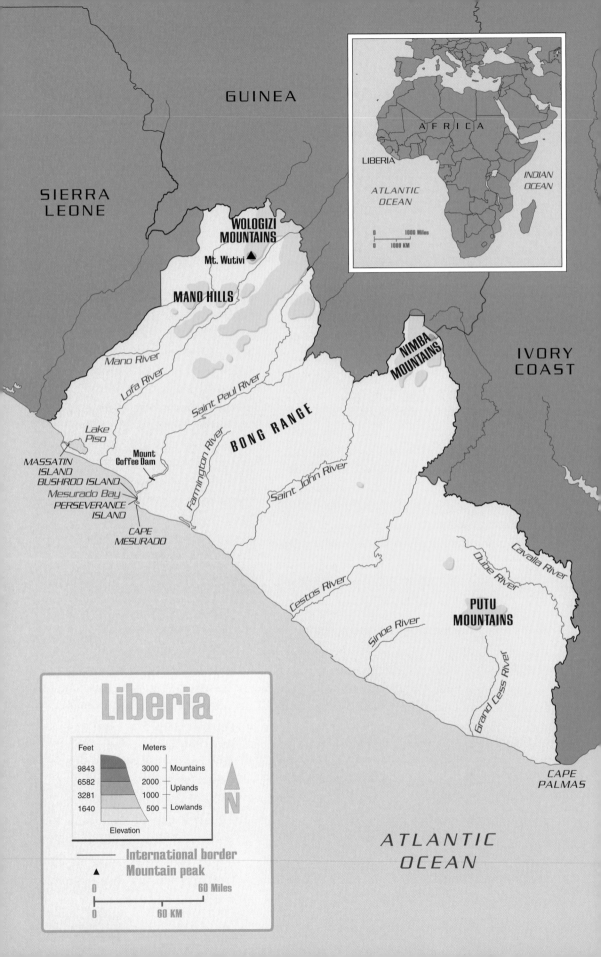

GUINEA

SIERRA
LEONE

WOLOGIZI
MOUNTAINS

Mt. Wutivi

MANO HILLS

Mano River

Lofa River

Saint Paul River

BONG RANGE

NIMBA
MOUNTAINS

IVORY
COAST

Lake
Piso

Mount
Coffee Dam

MASSATIN
ISLAND
BUSHROD ISLAND

Mesurado Bay
PERSEVERANCE
ISLAND

CAPE
MESURADO

Farmington River

Saint John River

Cestos River

Sinoe River

Dube River

Cavalla River

PUTU
MOUNTAINS

Grand Cess River

CAPE
PALMAS

AFRICA

LIBERIA

ATLANTIC
OCEAN

INDIAN
OCEAN

0   1000 Miles
0   1000 KM

ATLANTIC
OCEAN

Liberia

Feet	Meters	
9843	3000	Mountains
6582	2000	Uplands
3281	1000	
1640	500	Lowlands

Elevation

N

——— International border
▲ Mountain peak

0   60 Miles

0   60 KM

Climate

Lying just north of the equator, the hottest zone on earth, Liberia has a hot, wet climate. Winters are generally dry, with little rain. During winter, dry winds called harmattans often blow into Liberia from the Sahara Desert far to the north. In summer the weather is rainy, with high humidity (moisture in the air) that can make people feel sticky and uncomfortable. Temperatures in Liberia vary little seasonally. Year-round, average high temperatures hover around 90°F (32°C). In the evening, temperatures dip to about 70°F (21°C).

The rainy season runs from April to October, when rains often flood unpaved roads, turning them into small streams of water and mud. Liberians get a short break from the rain in late July and August, a time known as the middle dries. In Liberia's northwestern coastal areas, as much as 205 inches (521 centimeters) of rain fall every year. The southeastern coast receives less rain, about 100 inches (254 cm) per year. The nation's interior receives an average of 70 inches (178 cm) of annual rainfall.

COLLECTING LATEX

The raw material used to make rubber is a thick, white sap known as latex. To collect this fluid, rubber workers use sharp, long-handled tools to carve diagonal cuts in the bark of rubber trees. The latex flows slowly down these cuts and into small cups, which fill up after several weeks. Workers take the latex to a processing center, where it is mixed with water and chemicals and pressed into thick white sheets.

Latex is used to make tires, clothing, food packaging, and rubber seals for equipment, engines, and water systems. The process of tire making turns raw latex black. If the tires on your family's car stayed a natural color during processing, they would be white.

Natural Resources

Liberia has large mineral reserves, including iron ore, diamonds, gold, tin, hematite, magnetite, and bauxite. Most of these minerals are found in the hills of northern and central Liberia. Many foreign companies have built mines to extract the minerals and railroads to transport minerals to the coast for export (sale to other countries).

Liberia's fertile soil and climate allow for the growing of a wide range of crops and trees. Rubber trees provide latex. Timber, another valuable natural resource, is used for making furniture and other wooden items. Liberian farmers also grow rice, coffee, sugarcane, bananas, pineapples, mangoes, and coconut palms.

Experts believe that petroleum (crude oil) deposits might exist off Liberia's coast, but Liberia does not have the equipment or the skilled engineers to extract the oil. Discouraged by the unstable political situation of the late twentieth century, foreign oil companies have avoided investing in Liberia.

Environmental Issues

In recent decades, civil war has damaged Liberia's rain forests. Various factions in the conflict have carried out extensive logging, with no government oversight or regulation. The warring groups have sold the valuable wood to raise money and buy weapons. The result is deforestation—the destruction of vast stretches of forest.

With the destruction of forests, plants and animals have fewer places to live, and many species are in danger of extinction. For example, the pygmy hippopotamus, the western African chimpanzee, and the viviparous toad are all threatened with extinction. Deforestation causes other problems as well. Without the root systems of trees in place, fertile topsoil easily washes away in Liberia's heavy rains. Rivers fill up with mud, blocking river traffic.

Liberia's cities and towns face a variety of additional environmental problems. Some factories dump dangerous chemicals into rivers and coastal waters. Most people in Liberia do not have up-to-date bathrooms. They use rivers as sewers, polluting them with human and household waste. Along the coast, oil and other pollutants from sunken and damaged ships sometimes leak into ocean waters. In some places, groundwater (underground water) is polluted and not safe for

Logging and destruction from the Liberian civil war have harmed the country's rain forest.

drinking. Hard-pressed for money and technical know-how, the Liberian government has been unable to fight these problems or ease the country's extensive water pollution.

The Liberian government has made some efforts to protect its environment. In 1983 Liberia created Sapo National Park, a 505-square-mile (1,308 sq. km) reserve along the Sinoe River. The reserve is off-limits to settlement, construction, hunting, and farming. It provides a natural home for a wide variety of birds and land animals.

The UN has tried to protect Liberia's rain forests. In July 2003, the United Nations Security Council placed a ban on all timber trade with Liberia. In this way, the UN hoped to stop the illegal logging and selling of timber by Liberia's various factions. The UN announced that the ban would continue until Liberia established a government agency to supervise the harvest of its trees. Countries that buy timber from Liberia, in violation of the ban, must pay penalties to the UN.

Cities

Many Liberians live in rural villages in the country's interior. About 45 percent of Liberians make their homes in coastal urban areas.

MONROVIA (population 550,000) is the capital and largest city of Liberia. It lies along the sandy cape at the mouth of the Saint Paul River. African Americans from the United States founded Monrovia in 1822. They first named their town Christopolis (meaning "City of Christ") but then renamed it Monrovia after U.S. president James Monroe. The founders built a rectangular grid of streets and small houses based on architectural styles they had known at home in the United States.

In the early twentieth century, Monrovia became a shipping and industrial center for Liberia. The city attracted farmers from rural areas in search of jobs and a better standard of living, as well as merchants and traders from Lebanon in the Middle East and the southern Asian nation of India. In 1948 the United States provided funds and engineers to help build the city's main port on Bushrod Island, as well as the nearby Roberts International Airport, the country's largest airport.

Conflict in the late twentieth century brought widespread destruction to Monrovia. After the civil war, the city had no working electricity, water, or sewer systems. It had no regular garbage collection or street maintenance. Unemployed people—many of them war refugees—lived in overcrowded and unhealthy slums.

Modern-day Monrovia spreads across several islands separated by lagoons. Office and apartment buildings, hotels, and stores cover the tip of Cape Mesurado. The Executive Mansion, home of Liberia's president, rises above Capitol Hill, which is also home to the University of Liberia.

Once a grand port city, **Monrovia** has been ravaged by civil war and increasing poverty. The Liberian government is working to rebuild the city and to restore jobs and international trade.

Two bridges connect Cape Mesurado with Bushrod Island, a center of manufacturing, refining, and port activities.

On Independence Day (July 26) in 1998, Liberians celebrated the national holiday by putting a traffic light at the corner of Broad and Lynch streets in downtown Monrovia. The signal was the first traffic light to operate in the country since 1990, when civil war was raging. Although Monrovia has power lines, it has no working electrical plants. Any business or home that needs electricity must use private, gas-fired generators.

BUCHANAN (population 26,000), Liberia's second-largest city, lies on the central coast. In the early nineteenth century, a group of black Americans from Pennsylvania formed the Young Men's Colonization Society for the purpose of resettling in Africa. They sailed from the United States and founded the town in 1835. Originally called Grand Bassa, in 1841 the town was renamed for Thomas Buchanan, the first governor of Liberia.

The main economic activity in Buchanan is processing iron ore, the raw material used in steel production. Raw ore arrives in Buchanan by train from mines in the Nimba Mountains. In Buchanan the ore is polished and formed into small pellets, then shipped to factories around the world. Most of the residents of Buchanan were employed in the city's port or iron ore businesses before the civil war. But war closed down mining and railroad activity. Buchanan is linked by a road to Monrovia and by a railroad to the Ivory Coast.

HARBEL (population 18,000) lies about 30 miles (48 km) southeast of Monrovia on the Farmington River. Harbel became the center of the Liberian rubber industry with the arrival of the Firestone Tire and Rubber Company in 1926. The company planted rubber trees and built the city in the middle of an uninhabited rain forest. The company also built schools, houses for workers, a hospital, a power plant, a radio station, and the Liberian Institute of Tropical Medicine, where scientists researched cures for tropical diseases. The institute was abandoned during the civil war. Also during the war, in 1993, hundreds of civilians (nonsoldiers) died in Harbel during an attack by a rebel faction.

ROBERTSPORT (population 10,000), in Grand Cape Mount County, is named for Joseph Jenkins Roberts, the first black governor and first president of Liberia. The town is home to rice plantations and a fishing port. It also lies near two important Liberian tourist attractions, Lake Piso and Massatin Island. The civil war of the early 1990s devastated Robertsport. Although some rebuilding has begun, much of the city still lies in ruins.

Visit www.vgsbooks.com for links to websites with additional information about Monrovia—Liberia's capital—and other cities, as well Liberia's climate, plants, animals, and geography.

HISTORY AND GOVERNMENT

Historians think the earliest human settlement in Liberia took place in the thirteenth century. People fleeing conflict in the troubled kingdoms of Ghana to the east and Mali to the north pushed southward into the river valleys of Liberia. These settlers lived by hunting animals and gathering edible plants. Once they had established permanent villages, they began growing crops, including rice and millet.

Eventually, several different migrating groups settled throughout Liberia. In the fifteenth century, Mande-speaking peoples arrived from the north. Kwa speakers, including the Bassa and Dey peoples, populated the coast, mainly as fishers. The Kru and Grebo peoples lived in the east, while the Krahns inhabited the interior forests. The Mande group dominated northwestern Liberia, from the hills down to the sea. These groups traded with one another and with people in neighboring regions. They organized alliances to defend themselves against raids by outsiders.

Liberia's early settlers practiced a type of religion called animism.

Animism involves belief in the powerful spirits of the sky, mountains, forest, and other natural elements. Strong spiritual beliefs guided the people in their everyday lives.

⊙ Outside Traders

Starting in the fourteenth century, Portuguese navigators sailed along the coasts of western Africa in search of spices and other goods that were valuable in Europe. In 1461 Portuguese navigator Pedro de Sintra arrived off the coast of Liberia and sent men to explore and map the densely forested shoreline. The Portuguese named Cape Palmas in southeastern Liberia and marked it on their maps of the region. The Liberian coast held no natural harbors. Its shores featured high winds, rough seas, and dangerous sandbars. So Sintra and other Portuguese captains anchored their ships in the rough waters and sent sailors ashore in small boats to hunt animals and search for freshwater.

The Kru, who were capable sailors and navigators, were probably the first Liberians to trade with the Europeans. Kru boatmen rowed large canoes out to the anchored Portuguese ships and traded goods and food with the Europeans. Within a few years, Portugal had begun a busy trade with the Kru and several other groups in malagueta pepper, a sharp-flavored spice known as the grain of paradise. From this nickname, Europeans began to refer to the coast of Liberia as the Grain Coast.

In the sixteenth century, Mandingo traders began to travel to Liberia. The Mandingo were based in Mali. They came to Liberia to acquire ivory. This hard, creamy-white substance from the tusks of elephants and other animals was valued for carving and making sculptures. In exchange for ivory, Mandingo traders gave salt, iron tools, and cloth to the Liberians.

Equipped with powerful weapons, such as iron swords, the Mandingo took control of several territories in Liberia. They also captured some native Liberians and brought them to ports in western and northern Africa, where European traders purchased the captives and sold them as slaves. The Mandingo followed the Islamic religion, founded in Arabia in the seventh century A.D. Their wealth, power, and religion set them apart from the animist Liberians.

By the 1600s, the Grain Coast was attracting Portugal's trade rivals, including England, France, and Holland. By then Europeans had developed a thriving slave trade in western Africa. Slave traders took captive

In this drawing, African slaves aboard a slave ship are destined for the Americas. Slave traders captured some native Liberians and sold them into slavery.

Africans, captured either by Mandingo traders or in warfare, to slave depots on the western African coast. From there, European slavers crowded the captives into cargo holds on ships and transported them to plantations. These large farms were in the European colonies of North, Central, and South America. Many slaves ended up in the British colonies of North America in the 1600s and 1700s. In the late 1700s, thirteen of Britain's colonies rebelled during the American Revolution (1775–1783). During this time, slaves from Liberia were still arriving in what had become the United States.

A Return to Africa

By the early nineteenth century, the history of Liberia had become closely tied with the history of the United States. Soon after its war for independence, the young United States of America faced a dilemma. Although freedom had been the cornerstone of the American independence movement, the United States was also home to several million African slaves. In 1808 the United States banned the importation of new slaves into the country. Some states outlawed slavery. But slavery remained legal in many states, mostly in the American South.

Meanwhile, a large number of free African Americans (both freed slaves and the descendants of slaves) lived side by side with white Americans. This situation brought conflict between blacks and whites. Racial strife was common in many U.S. cities. Although some whites believed that blacks should and could be treated equally in the United States, other whites considered blacks to be undesirable outsiders. To many, it appeared that blacks and whites could never resolve their ethnic, social, and political differences.

To resolve the conflict, some white politicians proposed sending free black Americans to live in Africa. Many white Americans supported the idea. Opponents of slavery, for instance, thought that creating a new home for African Americans would provide an escape route for those blacks who were still in bondage. Slave owners, fearing that free blacks would inspire their slaves to revolt, also supported sending free blacks to Africa.

Many free blacks, too, saw settlement in Africa as a chance to escape racial discrimination and mistreatment in the United States. They wanted to create a new republic in Africa based on the ideals of individual liberty. But many other black Americans had no desire to move to Africa. Some even worried that the U.S. government might force them to move there.

In the late 1700s and early 1800s, small groups of free blacks settled in Sierra Leone, a British colony. In 1816 white Presbyterian minister Robert Finley founded the American Colonization Society (ACS), the first large-scale organization dedicated to seeking a new homeland in Africa for free African Americans. The cofounders of this group included the well-known politicians Henry Clay, President James Monroe, Bushrod Washington (a nephew of George Washington), Andrew Jackson (a future U.S. president), Francis Scott Key, and Daniel Webster.

The ACS created a constitution, and in 1818, U.S. and ACS officials journeyed to the Grain Coast to purchase land from African chiefs. The next year, the U.S. Congress granted $100,000 to the ACS. With this money, the ACS prepared its first emigrant ship, the *Elizabeth*. The ship sailed from New York in January 1820. It carried eighty-eight black emigrants and three white ACS agents.

Colonization and Early Struggles

The *Elizabeth* reached land at Sherbro Island in Sierra Leone. Soon after, an outbreak of yellow fever struck the ship, killing many passengers. The survivors remained in Sierra Leone to await another ship. A second ship, the *Nautilus*, reached Africa the next year. After collecting the survivors from the *Elizabeth* expedition, the *Nautilus* reached a small island in Mesurado Bay, which they named Perseverance (present-day Providence Island). In 1822 passengers aboard the *Alligator* arrived at a small plot of land acquired by ACS agents from King Peter, an African chief. Here the settlers founded Monrovia.

ESTABLISHING CHRISTIANITY

Many early settlers from the United States were missionaries, or dedicated church members determined to bring Christianity to the indigenous people of Liberia. With support from the Liberian government, Baptist, Methodist, and other Christian settlers built churches and religious schools in Liberia. In a further attempt to spread Christianity, the government outlawed all work on Sunday.

In 1824 the ACS formally named the colony Liberia—from the Latin word for "freedom." The colony consisted of a few dozen homes, made of wood and thatch gathered from the surrounding forest, and small fields cleared for the growing of corn and rice. Most of the settlers were Christians, who brought their religious traditions with them to Africa. They built churches and tried to convert the indigenous people to Christianity. The English-speaking settlers brought their language to their new home in Africa.

The new settlers, who came to be called Americo-Liberians, struggled with hunger, disease, and raids from local people. In 1825 and 1826, Jehudi Ashmun, a white American, negotiated with Liberian chiefs for more land for the colony. Ashmun also made peace treaties with groups that had attacked the settlements.

In addition to the ACS, other colonization societies founded more towns along the Liberian coast. For instance, the Young Men's Colonization Society in Pennsylvania created the town of Grand Bassa (modern Buchanan). Free blacks from Maryland established a colony at Cape Palmas in southeastern Liberia. Meanwhile, the U.S. Navy stopped slave ships along the western African coast, freed the captives, and took them to live in the new colony.

The colonists struggled to survive in their new land. Tropical diseases posed a constant threat, and just finding fresh drinking water was a daily challenge. The supply of fertile land for growing crops was very small. Indigenous fighters raided the tiny settlements, sometimes killing the colonists and destroying their property. Many colonists also suffered loneliness and homesickness. But gradually the settlements grew as more U.S. colonists arrived.

Independence

At first, the ACS appointed only white governors to rule Liberia. But in 1841, the ACS made Joseph Jenkins (J. J.) Roberts the colony's first black governor. Born in Virginia, Roberts had to deal with serious problems while governor. Other countries did not recognize Liberia as an independent state. Furthermore, its settlements had no organized military to defend themselves. This situation brought conflict with foreign traders, who refused to pay customs duties (taxes on goods brought into Liberia) or to obey the colony's regulations. When Liberian officials seized goods from uncooperative traders, foreign merchants responded by attacking Liberian towns.

To resolve these problems, Governor Roberts decided to prepare the colonists for full independence. He wanted to create a new nation that

SAVING THE SETTLEMENT

The Americo-Liberian settlers faced frequent and deadly attacks from the surrounding indigenous people of the Grain Coast. The settlers did their best to fend off these attacks, and many died in the attempt. According to legend, one defender saved her settlement almost by accident. The story says that one evening while Matilda Newport was out strolling and smoking her pipe on Ducor Hill, near Cape Mesurado, she saw a group of attackers moving toward the settlement. Walking past a loaded cannon, she touched her pipe to the cannon's fuse and set it off. Frightened by the surprising sound and smoke, the attackers fled immediately. Ever since this famous event, Liberia has celebrated December 1 as Matilda Newport Day.

The Back-to-Africa Movement

Although ACS operations ended with the Civil War, the idea of emigration from the United States to Africa did not die out completely. Taking up the cause in the 1920s was Marcus Garvey. An immigrant from the Caribbean island of Jamaica, Garvey organized and led the Universal Negro Improvement Association (UNIA). He believed that blacks would never be treated justly in the United States and called for the emigration of black Americans to Africa. He organized a steamship company, the Black Star Line, to carry out this task. But the UNIA suffered financial problems, and the Black Star Line failed. Garvey went to jail for mail fraud in 1925, and later, the U.S. government deported him to Jamaica. His call for emigration went unheeded among most African Americans, who preferred life in the United States to an uncertain future in Africa.

could write its own laws and organize a militia to defend itself, without interference from the ACS or the U.S. government. Men from various Americo-Liberian settlements met to create a constitution and a declaration of independence. (Women and indigenous people were not allowed to participate or vote for representatives.) On July 26, 1847, Liberia formally declared itself an independent nation. Roberts then won election as the nation's first president, for a term of two years.

He worked for diplomatic recognition of Liberia and had his first successes in 1848, when Great Britain and France formally recognized the republic. Many U.S. leaders, however, did not want to meet with black diplomats or make official ties with a black-led nation. So at first, the United States did not recognize Liberian independence.

Roberts was elected four times as president, serving for eight years. He signed treaties with neighboring countries to extend Liberian territory. He also founded Liberia College (later the University of Liberia) in the capital city of Monrovia. However, the young nation was no more than a strip of coastal settlements, with indigenous groups living independently in the interior. Under Stephen Allen Benson, Roberts's successor as president, Liberia annexed (took over) the region known as Maryland County in 1857.

The ACS continued to send colonists to Liberia until the U.S. Civil War (1861–1865). During the war, President Abraham Lincoln freed black slaves with the Emancipation Proclamation, a presidential order.

African American colonists wait for their ship to depart from the United States for the independent nation of Liberia in the mid-1800s.

In 1862 the United States decided to accept black diplomats, and it formally recognized Liberia's independence.

With the end of the war, the drive to colonize Liberia also ended. Amendments to the U.S. Constitution promised to protect the rights of African Americans. Encouraged by political changes at home, African Americans saw better opportunities for themselves in the United States than in distant Liberia.

Foreign Relations

In 1871 Edward Roye, a prosperous black merchant and immigrant from Ohio, was elected president of Liberia. Roye planned to construct new schools and roads. To raise money for these projects, he traveled to Great Britain to request loans from British banks. But when the Liberian treasury received much less money than the banks had actually loaned, other officials accused Roye of theft. When Roye returned from Great Britain, he found Liberians in revolt. He responded by issuing a proclamation that extended his term of office past the legal two years. In October 1871, Roye's opponents removed him from office by force. Facing a trial and prison, Roye tried to escape from the capital.

On February 12, 1872, he drowned while swimming to a British ship in Monrovia's harbor.

J. J. Roberts returned to serve two more presidential terms, from 1872 until 1876. Meanwhile, many nations in Europe were scrambling to claim colonies in western Africa and to build their own trade routes and ports. The British expanded their colony in Sierra Leone, while the French claimed the Ivory Coast. In 1883 Liberia began disputing its boundary with Sierra Leone. The conflict ended in 1885 with a treaty that established the Mano River as Liberia's northern border.

In 1884 Hilary Johnson became the first Liberian president to have been born in Liberia (his parents had emigrated from the United States). Two major political factions—the Republicans and the Whigs—had emerged by Johnson's term. While the Republicans sought close ties with Europe, the Whigs opposed European control and influence in Liberia. By the end of the nineteenth century, a group called the True Whig Party dominated the political scene. In 1892 Liberia made a treaty with France, which established Liberia's eastern border with the Ivory Coast.

Liberia tried to extend its authority to the peoples of the interior, in particular the Kru, the Gola, and the Grebo. The government allowed some indigenous groups to send representatives to the national legislature. Mainly, however, the indigenous Africans and the Americo-Liberians made up two

PRAISE FOR LIBERIA

The Reverend Daniel Peterson was a son of slaves who became a minister of the Bethel Church in Philadelphia in the mid-nineteenth century. He journeyed to parts of Liberia, including Monrovia, which he found to be a very pleasant place. "The whole view from this spot is beautiful," he wrote. "I must say that I never saw a more attractive place. Monrovia is perfectly healthy, and contains, at this time, three large stone Churches, an Academy, and High School, and all other conveniences required by a large town. . . . The people all look well, and have fine cattle, pigs, and goats. In fact, this place looks more like the Garden of Eden, than any place that I have ever seen or read about. . . . I can assure the reader, that the people in Liberia look as respectable [as those] in the United States, while they enjoy five times as much liberty, as ladies and gentlemen in the possession of all the comforts of life, and this in a nation of their own."

—Daniel H. Peterson, *The Looking-Glass*

distinct and separate social groups. Hostilities flared between the two groups. In 1893 Grebo forces staged a deadly attack on the Americo-Liberian town of Harper. The Liberian government sent a gunboat, the *Gorronomah*, to defeat the attackers. Later in the 1890s, Americo-Liberians fought with the Gola people. Both sides committed massacres.

New Struggles

In the early 1900s, Liberia was struggling economically. Since its founding, Liberia had tried to create a plantation-style economy, in which large farms produced agricultural goods for export. But Liberia had to compete for business with other European colonies in western Africa. Trade with Europe brought only a meager income, and Liberia had to borrow money from foreign countries to pay for its housing, roads, ports, and military forces. When Liberia found itself unable to pay its foreign debts, European nations threatened to attack and occupy the country. In 1912, after the election of President Daniel Edward Howard, European lenders saw that debt was preventing economic growth in Liberia. Seeking further opportunity for trade and investment, the United States and European nations agreed to extend a new loan. As a condition of the loan, U.S. and European advisers went to Liberia to supervise all payments made from the government treasury.

World War I (1914–1918) broke out in Europe. In 1917 Liberia joined the Allies (including Britain, France, and the United States), the nations fighting Germany and its allies during the war. German submarines blockaded Monrovia. This blocking of ship traffic devastated

This picture of **Liberian soldiers** was painted during World War I. Liberia fought as a member nation of the Allies during the war. In retaliation, the German navy blockaded the port at Monrovia, crippling Liberia's economy.

Liberia's economy, which depended on exports of raw materials to Europe. In 1918 World War I ended with a German defeat.

After the war, some companies still saw investment possibilities in Liberia. In 1926 the Firestone Tire and Rubber Company arrived in the country. The U.S. firm established a 1 million-acre (404,678-hectare) rubber tree plantation around the town of Harbel. In exchange for this land, the company agreed to pay Liberia rent of six cents an acre for ninety-nine years. Firestone also loaned Liberia more than $2 million to help the country pay its debts. The rubber plantation—the largest in the world—employed thousands of workers and bolstered the Liberian economy.

In 1930 Edwin Barclay became president of Liberia. Meanwhile, the Americo-Liberians were still clashing with indigenous peoples over issues such as taxes, territorial boundaries, and road tolls (use fees). For instance, the government charged a "hut tax" on indigenous groups, who had to pay a certain amount for each dwelling in their villages. This tax and others led to long-simmering resentment of the central government by the indigenous peoples of Liberia.

The Tubman Years

Germany's invasion of Poland touched off World War II (1939–1945) in Europe, The United States entered the war in 1941. As part of the war,

Liberian president Edwin Barclay (left) meets with U.S. president Franklin D. Roosevelt *(right)* during World War II. An Allied member nation, Liberia maintained close relations with the United States during and after the war.

Visit www.vgsbooks.com for links to websites with additional information about Liberia's history, colonization, the Back-to-Africa colonization movement, government, social and political unrest, and reforms.

the United States and its allies fought German forces in North Africa. With Liberia's cooperation, the United States built new port facilities in Monrovia as well as an airstrip at Robertsport. These facilities served as important supply points for U.S. troops in North Africa.

William V. S. Tubman, a government minister and a supreme court justice, became president of Liberia in 1944. Tubman wanted Liberia to play a more important role in world affairs. Under his leadership, Liberia officially entered World War II in 1944. In 1945, Liberia joined the new United Nations.

At home in Liberia, Tubman carried out important reforms and changes. During his presidency, the Liberian government expanded the public school system. It also extended the vote to women and to indigenous peoples. Tubman's administration encouraged indigenous people to take part in the Liberian government and opened government jobs to them. Tubman also allowed indigenous groups to follow their own laws—as opposed to federal laws—in their own territory.

William V. S. Tubman

The alliance between the United States and Liberia continued. The U.S. government saw Liberia as a key ally in the fight against Communism, a system of single-party rule in which the state owns all property and businesses. Communist nations, in particular the Soviet Union, were striving to gain allies throughout Africa. To fight this trend, the United States and Liberia signed an agreement, promising to aid each other in military conflicts in western Africa. The United States also built a communications post in Liberia to broadcast *Voice of America*, a pro-U.S. radio show, throughout Africa. President Tubman supported the United States by voting with U.S. officials on important issues that came before the United Nations. And in the early 1960s, the U.S.

Peace Corps sent volunteers to Liberia to help build new schools and other public facilities.

Profits from iron ore and rubber allowed the Liberian government to develop Monrovia. It built new water and sewer systems and hydro-electric plants on several rivers. New roads ran between the interior and the coast, allowing easier movement of goods to ports for shipment. Liberia also developed its ship registration industry. With this business, foreign merchant vessels could save taxes and fees in their home countries by registering with the Liberian government. Foreign investment increased, and Liberian planters exported crops such as coffee, oranges, and coconuts.

A Troubled Government

William Tubman was succeeded in 1971 by his vice president, William R. Tolbert, who came from a wealthy family of rice farmers. Tolbert continued the improvements and new investment of his predecessor. But many people in Liberia accused his administration of accepting bribes and fixing elections. In addition, Tolbert angered the United States by establishing diplomatic ties with the Soviet Union, China, and Cuba—all Communist rivals of the United States. Tolbert's administration grew increasingly unpopular. When Tolbert declared an increase in the government-controlled price of rice in 1979, deadly riots broke out in Monrovia.

For many indigenous people, Tolbert was a symbol of Americo-Liberians' unjust domination of Liberian political and business life. In 1980 a group of military leaders, headed by Samuel K. Doe, a member of the Krahn people, overthrew Tolbert's government. Tolbert was killed in the fighting. Doe then ordered the execution of thirteen of Tolbert's ministers. Doe and sixteen coplotters formed the People's Redemption Council to govern the country.

Doe was a suspicious and intolerant leader who wanted the Krahn people to dominate Liberia's government. To silence his opponents, he shut down several newspapers and punished critics with imprisonment and public executions. He governed as a dictator, a ruler with absolute power. Doe banned political parties and refused to hold elections. But he also mended relations with the United States, which supported his government with funds and loans for development. In 1985 the United States persuaded Doe to revise Liberia's constitution and hold an election. Doe and his supporters swept the election, which many Liberians believed had been rigged.

Further trouble occurred when one of Doe's ministers, Thomas Quiwonkpa, left the government and formed a private army in Sierra Leone. Quiwonkpa invaded Liberia, but Doe's forces captured and killed him in

Monrovia. Then the Krahn-dominated Liberian army then invaded Quiwonkpa's homelands in Nimba County.

The Taylor Regime

Another member of the People's Redemption Council was Charles Taylor. After a dispute with Doe, Taylor moved to the United States for a time but then returned to the Ivory Coast. The president of the Ivory Coast, Félix Houphouët-Boigny, allowed Taylor to gather weapons and soldiers for an attack on Doe's government. Taylor formed an army called the National Patriotic Front of Liberia (NPFL).

In 1989 the NPFL invaded Liberia and made rapid progress until reaching Monrovia. There, Doe's forces made a stand, while the NPFL broke into two factions, one under the command of Taylor and the other led by Taylor's rival, Prince Johnson.

A militia commanded by Johnson captured Monrovia and killed Doe. Civil war then erupted as Johnson fought Taylor for control of the country. Another faction, the United Liberation Movement of Liberia (ULIMO), was organized in Sierra Leone in 1991. This group of Krahn and Mandingo fighters fought against both factions of the NPFL.

Charles Taylor

A brutal civil war erupted, with armies made up of followers of Taylor, Johnson, and Alhaji Kromah, leader of ULIMO. Each faction's armies roved through the countryside, looting and destroying villages suspected

LINKS TO LIBERIA

Many refugees of the Liberian civil war have moved to the United States. They enjoy temporary protected status (TPS). This status allows people who have fled civil war, environmental disaster, or the threat of political violence to take temporary shelter in the United States. Some Liberians in the United States have taken steps to become permanent U.S. residents.

Liberian refugees have made their homes in several large U.S. cities, including Philadelphia, Washington, D.C., and New York. Liberians in the United States have also formed many associations to keep in touch with their home country and to work for a better future for Liberia. These groups include the Union of Liberian Associations and the Liberian Studies Association, which organizes student exchanges between Liberia and the United States. The Grand Gedeh Association has chapters in several U.S. states. It sends medical and school supplies to the people of Grand Gedeh County, Liberia.

In Liberian English, the word *palaver* refers to a meeting of chiefs or officials to decide important questions. But *palaver* can also mean "dispute." A popular term for the recent civil war in Liberia is the Big Palaver.

of helping opponents. Thousands of villagers fled the violence. Others were murdered or given arms and forced to fight for one faction or another.

In 1993 the United Nations arranged a cease-fire and an agreement called the Cotonou Accord, which established a five-member Council of State to govern Liberia. The cease-fire did not hold, however, and fighting soon resumed. Then ULIMO broke into rival Krahn and Mandingo factions, and several more factions formed as well. In August 1996, the various factions signed another agreement, the Abuja II Accord. Ruth Perry won election as head of the Council of State, becoming the first female head of state in Africa. Meanwhile, the fighting had devastated Liberia's cities and economy. More than 200,000 Liberians had lost their lives, and thousands more had fled the country.

An election in 1997 made Charles Taylor president of Liberia. Taylor governed as a dictator, sending thousands of his opponents to their deaths and allowing his army, made up largely of Gio and Mano

Krahn fighters attack Taylor-backed NPFL forces on a Monrovian street during the Liberian civil war in 1996.

Homeless civilians wait for much-needed food, water, and medical relief during the Liberian civil war. The war caused hardship for civilians in Liberia and in neighboring Sierra Leone.

people, to massacre members of rival groups. Taylor also supported a rebellion in neighboring Sierra Leone by giving weapons to Sierra Leonean rebels in exchange for diamonds mined in Sierra Leone. The diamonds went directly into the pockets of Taylor's ministers, who then sold the gems on the world market for a profit. In response, the UN imposed a ban on diamond exports from Liberia as well as a ban on arms sales to the country.

In 1999 opponents of Taylor's government organized Liberians United for Reconciliation and Democracy (LURD) in northern Liberia. Another rebel group, the Movement for Democracy in Liberia (MDL), emerged in the south. These groups staged hit-and-run attacks on government troops and offices and committed acts of terror and violence in Liberia's coastal cities. On June 17, 2003, LURD, MDL, and Taylor's government signed a cease-fire in Accra, Ghana. In the same year, Sierra Leone charged Taylor as a war criminal for his support of the rebellion in that country. He resigned in August and fled to Nigeria, where the government offered him refuge.

In the fall of 2003, LURD, MDL, and members of Taylor's government signed a peace agreement, and the United Nations sent a peacekeeping force to Liberia. In October the factions selected businessman Gyude Bryant to be chairman of a National Transition Government. Liberian voters also elected a new seventy-six-member Legislative Assembly.

The National Transition Government tried to disarm rebel factions. It also wanted to attract foreign aid and investment, to oversee reconstruction, and to put Liberia on the road to recovery after many years of civil war. In October 2005, the nation voted on a new president and legislature.

In November 2005, Ellen Johnson-Sirleaf claimed victory over former Liberian soccer star George Manneh Weah in a heated presidential runoff election. If confirmed, Johnson-Sirleaf—Africa's first democratically elected woman president—vows to unite and rebuild the nation.

◉ Government

Liberia governs itself under a revised constitution passed on January 6, 1986. According to the constitution, all adult citizens are eligible to vote. However, the constitution declares that "only persons who are Negroes or of Negro descent" may become citizens of Liberia.

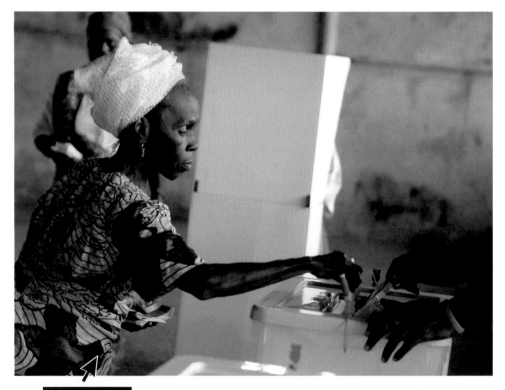

A woman votes for one of twenty-two candidates during the 2005 Liberian presidential election on October 11. The election was the first free election after fourteen years of civil war.

The president of Liberia serves a six-year term. The president appoints a cabinet (a team of advisers), which must be confirmed by the Senate. The president also appoints top officials to govern Liberia's fifteen counties. On the local level, residents of cities and towns elect mayors. Town chiefs preside in indigenous villages. In some villages, a village council chooses the chief. In other villages, the job of chief is passed down from father to son.

The Liberian legislature is divided into a twenty-six-seat Senate, whose members serve nine-year terms, and a sixty-four-member House of Representatives, whose members serve six-year terms. Members of the legislature are elected on a system of proportional representation. Under this system, each political party sends a certain number of representatives to the legislature, based on the percentage of votes it wins in the election.

Liberia's justice system is led by a Supreme Court. The court meets in Monrovia to decide issues of national scope and to interpret the constitution. Liberia also has appeals courts, criminal courts, and county courts. The indigenous people have their own court system for trying criminals and resolving local disputes.

Visit www.vgsbooks.com for links to election and government information from the U.S. Liberian Embassy and the Liberian newspapers *The Liberian Times* and *The Analyst.*

THE PEOPLE

Liberia has not carried out an official census—a count of its people—since 1986. But current estimates place the population at 3.5 million and population growth at about 2.9 percent a year. At this rate of growth, Liberia will reach a population of 6.1 million in the year 2025. About 45 percent of Liberia's people live in urban areas along the seacoast.

○ Ethnic Groups

Liberia is a patchwork quilt of sixteen different African ethnic groups. The largest group is the Kpelle, who live in central and western Liberia. From largest to smallest, the remaining groups are the Bassa, Grebo, Gio, Kru, Mano, Lorma, Mandingo, Kissi, Gola, Krahn, Vai, Gbandi, Mende, Belle, and Dey. By most estimates, the Americo-Liberians, defined as descendants of nineteenth-century settlers from North America, form only about 5 percent of the population.

Liberia also has a small population of Lebanese and East Indian people, whose ancestors came to the country in the early twentieth century as

merchants and traders. Most Liberian people of foreign descent live in the cities. A small community of Europeans, most of them employed by foreign companies and governments, also lives in urban Liberia.

Over half a million Liberians fled the country during the civil war of the early 1990s. These refugees scattered to neighboring countries, to Europe, and to North America. Many of them were professionals—doctors, lawyers, engineers, and skilled workers—who left the country out of fear for their lives and the safety of their families. As Liberia returns to stability, some refugees who fled to neighboring African countries have returned to Liberia. Many overseas refugees, however, have made a new life in their adopted countries and are reluctant to return.

Rural and Urban Life

Life in Liberian villages runs at a slow pace. People live in small homes made of wood, tin, or mud bricks and roofed with tin or thatch (a mat of plant materials). Most homes have no electricity or running water.

Villagers walk from place to place or use canoes to travel up and down rivers. Most villagers work as subsistence farmers, growing just enough food to feed their families. In good years, farmers may have a small surplus (extra crops) to sell. During the harvest season, farmers hold festivals and celebrations that include music and dancing. Visitors come from distant places to join the celebrations.

City life is more fast paced. People live in homes made of wood, brick, or concrete. They work in shops, factories, and offices. City life has many challenges. Residents often struggle with unemployment, food shortages, and violent crime. The poorest city dwellers make their homes in shanty-towns. Their houses are built from scrap metal, discarded boards, and concrete blocks, with no toilets or clean running water.

During the civil war, life in the cities got even harder. Street fighting disrupted daily life and made it impossible for shopkeepers and street vendors to stock food and other necessities. Schools and hospitals closed, public transportation broke down, and many city dwellers lost their jobs. Many people fled to temporary refugee camps, with no jobs, no way to raise food, and little money. The war also made orphans of many children, who had to beg, steal, and scavenge to survive in battle-scarred city streets.

Liberia is struggling to repair the damage and return to normalcy. Life in the cities remains a difficult daily challenge, however. Public transportation systems remain closed, so most people walk or take private taxis to get around. Few people own cars, but those who do often can't find gasoline to fill their tanks. Cities do not collect garbage, so people take

CHANGING TRADITIONS

In earlier centuries, indigenous Liberian households included a husband and one or more wives, as well as children and an extended family of grandparents and single relatives. Families built separate huts for living, hosting guests, and housing sacred religious objects. Each village had a palaver hut, where men met to discuss and resolve problems.

Women did the work of planting and harvesting and of caring for the home and children. They also took surplus crops—fruit, palm oil, and plantains—to sell at local markets. With the money they earned, women bought household supplies such as farm tools, utensils, cooking pots, and cloth. They taught their daughters to farm, cook, and sew. Men and boys hunted, cleared the land by cutting and burning trees, and built fences around their villages. Many of these roles and traditions changed when rural people began moving to Liberian cities in the mid-twentieth century.

Fresh well water is precious to Liberians, who have little or no safe running water and whose wells are threatened by contamination.

DANGEROUS WATER

Liberia has no system of water reservoirs or a public water supply. People get their water from rivers, streams, and public wells. Monrovia has more than five thousand wells, but these wells pose a serious health danger to the people who use them. They can be contaminated by garbage falling in from the street. Polluted well water can also transmit serious diseases such as cholera.

To guard the water supply, health workers must walk from well to well and deposit chlorine into the water. The chemical chlorine kills most of the germs in the water, making it safe to drink. However, rainwater can quickly dilute chlorine. Sunlight also weakens it. Chlorinating the water supply in Liberian cities is a difficult and endless task.

their household waste to vast dumps, where it is burned. Electrical generating plants shut down during the war, so a family wanting light or electric current must use a gas-fired generator.

Liberian city dwellers combat these hardships with the help of close friendships and family ties. Despite the problems they face, they still enjoy a range of leisure activities. Movie theaters show U.S. and other foreign films, and cookshops (restaurants) sell reasonably priced meals. Nightclubs and discos play dance music into the small hours of the night. Street markets are popular places for trading news and gossip, while churches provide a focus for spiritual life and social activities.

Education

Before U.S. settlers arrived, indigenous people trained their children in hunting, farming, and other skills needed for survival. They passed down history and wisdom orally—by word of mouth.

This **Liberian school** reopened shortly after the civil war. The Liberian government and world relief agencies continue to work to rebuild the country's educational system.

The Americo-Liberians developed an educational system based on U.S. models. They opened schools and universities, such as Liberia College, founded in Monrovia in 1863. Christian settlers founded Cuttington University College in Monrovia in 1889. The Americo-Liberians also ran missionary schools. They were designed to educate indigenous children and to teach them about Christianity.

After World War II, the Tubman administration expanded Liberia's educational system. The government built new public elementary, secondary, teacher-training, and job-training schools. Missionary schools continued to operate in indigenous areas. Both public and missionary schools used English as the language of instruction. As in the United States, children attended six years of elementary school, followed by three years of junior high and three years of high school. Especially in cities, the majority of school-age children attended school. Many rural areas, however, had no schools. Instead of attending school, many rural children worked on family farms.

The civil war that began in 1989 nearly destroyed Liberia's educational system. Warfare damaged or destroyed school buildings. Sometimes rebel factions took over schools and used them as military headquarters. Rebels also forced many children to join their ranks and take part in the fighting. Many teachers in public and missionary schools scattered to neighboring countries as refugees.

With the end of the civil war, Liberian schools are still recovering from the damage. By law, young people must attend school from six to sixteen years of age. Only about half of all children actually attend school, however. In the cities, many children attend only a few years of school before dropping out. Many children in rural areas have no school nearby or transportation to bring them to one. But at rubber plantations, children of rubber workers can attend company-run schools.

Because of the overall low rates of school attendance, few people in Liberia learn to read or write. The nation's literacy rate (percentage of people who can read and write) is only about 25 percent among young and old alike.

Health Care

After the civil war, about a million Liberians found themselves living in refugee camps. The United Nations built some of these camps, while church groups and private charities built others. The camps were meant as temporary shelters, but many became permanent homes. People there lived in large tents,

Liberians receive rations of food at a **refugee camp** in the late 1990s. Many of these temporary camps remain open in the country.

without proper health care, bathrooms, or schools. Disease was common in the camps.

Even in the cities of Liberia, the public health system broke down completely. Garbage and sewage collected in the streets, leading to outbreaks of disease such as dysentery and cholera. Warfare had demolished many hospitals and clinics, and doctors and nurses fled the country.

As of 2004, fewer than one hundred doctors were working in Liberia. No functioning water or sewer systems, no working hospitals, and very few medical clinics of any kind existed. Less than 10 percent of the population had access to health care. Infant mortality rates—the number of babies who die within a year of birth—stood at 150 per 1,000, an extremely high number. The average life expectancy for a Liberian was just 42 years, one of the lowest averages in the world.

Several diseases are common in Liberia. These include malaria, passed by the bite of mosquitoes, which causes high fever and sleepiness and in some cases death. Smallpox, measles, yellow fever, and tuberculosis also flourish in Liberia. Immunization (injection of disease-preventing drugs) can fight these diseases, but the country has a shortage of clinics, no immunization program, and no stocks of the needed drugs.

Like many nations, Liberia is struggling with HIV, or human immunodeficiency virus, which causes the condition known as AIDS

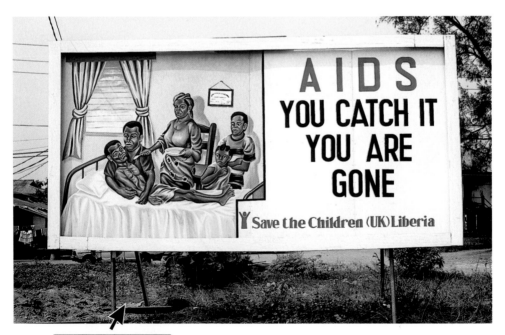

A health-care billboard outside of Monrovia, Liberia, warns of the danger of AIDS. Despite AIDS-prevention campaigns like this one, rates of AIDS and other diseases remain high in Liberia.

(acquired immunodeficiency syndrome). HIV weakens the human body's immune system, allowing a wide range of illnesses to attack the infected person. Several foreign aid and church organizations run HIV-prevention programs in Liberia. These programs teach people how to prevent exposure to HIV, which is primarily passed through intravenous drug use and sexual contact.

Despite prevention programs, approximately 8 percent of Liberia's adult population is HIV positive (infected with the virus). About 5,000 Liberians die from AIDS each year. The presence of other deadly diseases, such as yellow fever and cholera, worsens the AIDS picture in Liberia, since people infected with HIV die more easily of these illnesses. Many Liberian families have lost one or both parents to AIDS, and thousands of children have become orphans with little or no means to support themselves.

Visit www.vgsbooks.com for links to websites with additional information about the people of Liberia, their ethnic groups, rural and city life, and their educational and health-care systems.

CULTURAL LIFE

Despite warfare and poverty, Liberia is a land of cultural vitality. The nation's mix of ethnic groups—originating in Africa, the United States, and elsewhere—and the diversity of indigenous cultures have brought the country a great variety of visual arts, crafts, language, music, and media. Liberian cities are vibrant and ever changing. But rural villages have remained isolated, allowing centuries-old traditions to endure.

◉ Language and Literature

Before the arrival of U.S. colonists, Liberia's different indigenous groups spoke many different languages, including Kwa, Mande, Gola, Kissi, and Vai. None of the languages was written down, however. Although some Mandingo traders could write Arabic—a language originating in the Middle East—the vast majority of Liberian people lived without letters, books, or newspapers. People handed down information orally—through storytelling and song. In this way, people passed on important myths, family history, and ideas.

Settlers from the United States brought American English to Liberia in the nineteenth century. Since these settlers created the nation's government, they made English the country's official language. In modern times, government officials, teachers, businesspeople, and radio and TV broadcasters all use English in their day-to-day work. But many indigenous Liberians primarily speak an indigenous language and use English only as a second language. Many Liberians also speak pidgin English—a mixture of English and native languages. This pidgin language allows people from different ethnic groups to communicate with one another.

Since many Liberians never attend school or do so for only a few years, most Liberians—75 percent—cannot read or write. But illiteracy does not stop communication among the Liberian groups. In many places, people send messages from village to village by sounding drums. Professional storytellers also work in Liberian villages, passing on history and religious beliefs.

The Writings of the Vai

The Vai are the only Liberian indigenous people who have created a written form of their language. Originally the Vai, like other indigenous groups, had no alphabet or writing. But a member of this group, Dualu Bukele, created a Vai alphabet in the early nineteenth century. Written Vai has 240 characters, which stand for combinations of sounds. The Vai use this alphabet to keep records, and village elders pass down the writing system to children.

English-speaking Liberian writers have been describing the country's unique history and culture since the mid-nineteenth century. Edward Blyden, who was born in Saint Thomas, Virgin Islands, moved to Monrovia in the 1850s to pursue his goal of becoming a clergyman. Blyden was an able linguist, historian, and educator who served as Liberia's secretary of state during the 1860s. He was a leading voice for pan-Africanism—the movement to unify all Africans—and promoted native African customs, dress, and ways of thought. Blyden expressed these views in several important books, including *A Voice from Bleeding Africa, Liberia's Offering*, and *Christianity, Islam, and the Negro Race*.

A leading Liberian poet of the twentieth century, Bai T. Moore served in William V. S. Tubman's government of the 1940s. He is best known for writing a short novel, *Murder in the Cassava Patch*. He published his poetry in a collection called *Ebony Dust* and a series of Liberian folktales in *Chips from the African Story Tree*. Gabriel Williams, a noted journalist, wrote about the Liberian civil war in *Liberia: The Heart of Darkness*. After receiving death threats for his articles about Liberia's armed factions, Williams fled the country in 1993. Wilton Sankawulo is a professor of English and a novelist who served as chair of the Council of State in 1995–1996. His works include the novels *Sundown at Dawn: A Liberian Odyssey* and *The Rain and the Night*, as well as a biography, *Tolbert of Liberia*.

Edward Blyden

◉ Religion

Liberia has a great diversity of religious beliefs. Many indigenous people believe in spirits of the rivers and forest. They find power and magic in the earth's natural forces—a type of religious practice known as animism. Animist Liberians also believe that the spirits of their ancestors reside among them. Many rural families build small dwellings that house sacred objects and charms, which are used to gain favor with natural and ancestral spirits.

Indigenous people hold religious celebrations in the spring—during the planting of new crops—and after the fall harvest. They perform rituals to welcome newborns into the world, to celebrate weddings, and to accompany funerals. Ceremonies that honor important people, such as chiefs, can last over several days of music, feasting, and dancing. About 40 percent of Liberians hold animist beliefs.

Another 40 percent of Liberians attend Christian churches. Christianity arrived in 1822 with Lott Carey, a Baptist minister who came with the first settlers from the United States and built Liberia's first Christian church. Americo-Liberians also welcomed U.S. religious teachers—women and men, black and white—who traveled to the interior. These missionaries set up clinics and schools and tried to convert indigenous people to Christianity. In many places, the missionary schools were the only means for young Liberians to learn to read, write, and train for a profession. By the end of the twentieth century, the majority of the Kru, Grebo, Krahn, Belle, Kpelle, and Bassa people were practicing Christians.

Christian schoolchildren pray at a large service in Monrovia, Liberia. Brought by American colonists, Christian beliefs have a long history in the country.

A mosque, an Islamic house of worship *(background)*, **burns** following riots in Monrovia, Liberia, in 2004. Tensions between rival factions erupted in violence that year, disrupting a UN disarmament campaign.

Islam, the faith of the seventh-century Arab prophet Muhammad, came with the Mandingo traders who traveled regularly between Liberia and North Africa. The Mandingo converted a large number of Vai people to Islam. In the late nineteenth century, some Lebanese traders, who also practiced Islam, moved to Liberia. In modern times, Islamic people (also called Muslims) make up about 20 percent of Liberia's population. Some members of this community are calling for the government to allow Islamic courts. These courts would decide matters of marriage and divorce, family law, and inheritance according to Islamic custom.

◉ Art and Architecture

The skilled artists of Liberia work in a variety of media and materials. People use many artistic creations in public festivals and religious rituals. Liberia is best known for elaborate masks carved from ebony, cherrywood, mahogany, or walnut and decorated with leather, cloth, palm fiber, dyes, and yarn. Mende men wear the *bgini*, a mask of cloth and leopard skin, at ceremonial occasions such as the crowning of a new chief. Young women and men of some societies wear masks during their initiation into adulthood.

Several indigenous groups have perfected a "lost wax" method to create earrings, bracelets, necklaces, and anklets. In this process, the artist crafts a wax model of the piece. The artist then forms a clay mold around the model, heats the wax to make it melt away, and fills the hollow space with molten (melted) bronze or brass. After the metal cools and hardens, the clay mold is broken away to reveal the finished piece, which is then filed and polished.

The indigenous people of Liberia also create baskets and mats from reeds and palm fronds, small sculpted figures out of wood and ivory, and woven cloth in traditional patterns and colors. Skilled leatherworkers create shoes and clothing, and wood carvers fashion useful household items, such as plates, bowls, cups, pitchers, eating utensils, chairs, and beds.

THE SARCASTIC MASK

The Mende, Vai, and other groups make fun with the *gongoli*, a large and comical wooden mask. Gongolis are made to look like real people, such as chiefs and village elders, but the masks are often unflattering, with exaggerated facial features and expressions.

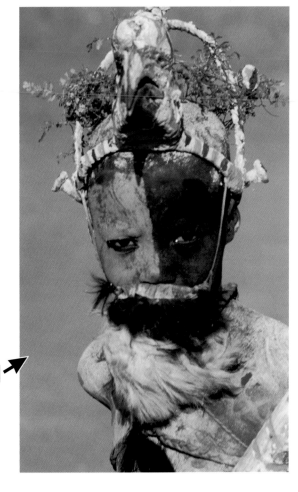

A Kissi boy wears a mask during a traditional festival. Many of Liberia's native peoples create colorful and elaborate masks for rites of passage, ceremonies, and celebrations.

A young girl stands between **murals** on a doorway in Monrovia, Liberia. Urban artists, such as Vanjah Richards, have popularized the art form in Liberia's cities.

Liberia had a lively urban art scene before the civil war of the 1990s. Monrovia was home to art galleries and studios, and several noted western African painters and sculptors worked in the capital. Vanjah Richards, a popular mural painter whose works appeared in public spaces and buildings, was killed during the fighting.

Urban architecture in Liberia has been influenced by settlers from the United States. In the nineteenth century, settlers built homes that mirrored those they had known in the American South. Such homes were made of sawn wood and had wide porches, bay windows, and gabled roofs. In the twentieth century, Monrovian builders constructed a few high-rise apartment and office buildings. They made government and other public buildings out of concrete and glass, in a plain boxy style.

Music

Among the indigenous people of Liberia, music accompanies every type of village celebration and important event. Music is a vital part of religious and initiation ceremonies. People also play music to celebrate births and marriages and to accompany funerals. Once completed, the fall rice harvest brings out village musicians.

From time to time, Kpelle people combine music, dance, and storytelling in a festival known as Meni-pelee. Drummers gather, and villagers form a circle to watch dancers. A master of ceremonies calls out the musical numbers and encourages the performers as well as audience members, who sometimes join in to sing familiar songs.

The most common musical instruments in Liberia are drums, which come in all shapes and sizes. The big goblet drum, placed on the ground while played, is made of animal skin stretched tight over a solid wood frame. The hourglass drum has two heads and is held at the side of the body. The performer raises and lowers the drum's pitch, or tone, by squeezing ropes strung between the heads. During performances, drummers use their hands or sticks to beat out complex rhythms, while a master drummer sets down a basic steady beat. People use the largest, deepest-toned drums to communicate with neighboring villages.

Another popular instrument is the xylophone, made of a series of hollowed-out logs. When struck with a mallet, the largest logs produce low tones, and smaller ones make high tones. People also play hollow gourds, which are struck or shaken. Beads strung along the gourds' surface make buzzing sounds. A zither is made of a series of strings stretched within a wooden frame. People also play wind instruments, made of rhinoceros horns or ivory tusks pierced by a series of holes.

Liberian boys practice drumming on a Monrovian street. **Traditional drums** remain popular in Liberia.

In the cities, many musicians combine traditional African rhythms with modern instruments such as electric guitars and drum machines. In Monrovia's nightclubs and discotheques feature a popular African-style known as highlife. This upbeat music features electric guitars and keyboards, drums, and singers who blend traditional African melodies with a modern dance beat.

Religious music is also important in Liberia. In church, worshippers often use the call-and-response style of singing. In this musical style, a leader sings a line and other singers repeat or answer the leader. This style of music originated in western Africa. It traveled to the United States with slaves, then went back to the coast of Liberia with U.S. settlers.

Media and Communications

Liberia's modern mass communications began with the nation's first radio station, which went on the air in 1927. Several FM and AM stations broadcast in Liberia. In many parts of the country, these stations provide the only news from the outside world. A Swiss company, the Fondation Hirondelle, operates Star Radio. It transmits programs in English, French, and fourteen indigenous languages. One television station, ELTV, broadcasts in Monrovia. While only a small percentage of households have televisions, many more Liberian households have battery-operated radios.

THE FINGER SNAP

When one Liberian greets another, an unusual kind of handshake occurs. One person extends a thumb and middle finger to grasp the middle finger of another person, then snaps the finger, as if snapping one's own finger. This greeting is said to come from the days of slave trading, when slave raiders and merchants would mark their slaves by deliberately breaking their middle fingers. Freed slaves who settled in Liberia turned the cruel practice into a friendly greeting.

Liberian newspapers date to the *Liberia Herald*, founded by U.S. settlers in 1826. Newspapers in modern Liberia are a lively forum for news and opinion. The papers offer detailed coverage of politics, and many Liberians take a deep and personal interest in political news. Editors and writers have sometimes paid a heavy price for articles that criticize the government, however. Recent Liberian governments have closed down newspapers and thrown journalists into prison.

No films have been made in Liberia. But some Liberians living in other countries have made documentary movies about the nation's history and modern conflicts. For example, in 2002 Nancee Oku Bright, a Liberian living in New

York, chronicled Liberian history and the horrors of the nation's civil war in *Liberia: America's Stepchild*. Gerald K. Barclay, another refugee who fled the civil war for the United States, documented his family's flight from Liberia's conflict in *Liberia: The Love of Liberty Brought Us There*.

At the start of the twenty-first century, Liberia had two Internet service providers and about five hundred Internet users. Since few Liberians own computers and electricity is scarce, most users rely on computers found at universities or hotels. In Monrovia a few Internet cafés have opened. There, users can rent computer time for e-mail, Web surfing, or chat.

◉ Sports and Leisure

The most popular sport in Liberia is soccer (called football in Liberia). Local teams belong to the Liberia Football Association and compete for the Barclay Championship Shield, the national championship. Liberia also sends a national team to compete in international events, such as the World Cup and the Summer Olympic Games. Several Liberians have signed professional contracts to play in European soccer leagues. Liberia also has a national basketball team.

Tondo Georges *(right)* of the Liberian national soccer team tackles a player from Guinea's national team during a game in the early 2000s. Soccer is the most popular sport in Liberia.

Liberians enjoy board games such as backgammon and checkers. Another popular board game is Mancala, played with stones, seeds, or marbles. Before the civil war, some foreign companies maintained golf courses and tennis courts in Liberia, but warfare shut them down.

Holidays

Liberia observes a number of public holidays. February 11 is Armed Forces Day. National Redemption Day, on April 12, recognizes the coup of 1980. March 15 is celebrated as the birthday of Joseph Jenkins Roberts, the first black governor and first president of Liberia. Liberia's independence is celebrated on July 26. Thanksgiving comes on the first Thursday in November, and the nation observes the birthday of President William V. S. Tubman on November 29, also known as Goodwill Day.

Rural festival dancers

Liberian Christians celebrate the holidays of Easter and Christmas, while Muslims observe the holy month of Ramadan with fasting and prayer. In the countryside, Liberians celebrate planting and the harvest with lively festivals, featuring dance, music, feasting, and storytelling.

Food

Rice is the primary food of Liberia. Everyone eats rice at nearly every meal. Also popular is cassava, a root crop grown by many households in small gardens. Liberians also enjoy sweet potatoes, plantains (similar to bananas), sweet corn, cabbage, eggplant, and okra. They eat a wide variety of fruits, including grapefruit, mangoes, oranges, bananas, and watermelons. They use hot red peppers and ginger to season foods. People pound and cook the flesh of palm nuts to make palm butter, as a base for a meat and vegetable stew. Many families cook outside on a small cookstove or a fire pit built with heavy stones.

Meat, including pork, beef, goat, and chicken, is sometimes available in city markets. In rural areas, hunters bring home wild game from the surrounding forest. People serve goat soup at formal occasions and

Visit www.vgsbooks.com for links to websites with additional information about the culture of Liberia, including arts and architecture, religions, foods, popular sports, and more.

JOLLOF RICE

Jollof rice is a tasty, traditional western African dish.

½ cup vegetable oil

2 pounds chicken or pork, sliced into small pieces

½ cup chopped yellow onions

½ cup chopped green peppers

½ teaspoon ground ginger

1 16-ounce can whole tomatoes

2 6-ounce cans tomato paste

1 cup water

½ teaspoon thyme

1 teaspoon crushed red pepper

1 pinch salt

1 pinch pepper

2 cups uncooked white rice

1. Add ¼ cup oil to a large frying pan and heat over medium heat.
2. Cook meat in oil until lightly browned on all sides.
3. Remove meat from pan and drain on paper towel. Set aside.
4. Add ¼ cup oil to a medium saucepan and heat over medium heat.
5. Add onions and peppers and cook until tender, about 5 minutes.
6. Stir in ground ginger.
7. Add tomatoes, reduce heat to medium-low, and simmer for 5 minutes.
8. Add tomato paste, water, thyme, crushed red pepper, and salt and pepper.
9. Add cooked meat, cover, and simmer for 20 minutes.
10. While meat and vegetables are cooking, cook rice according to directions on the package.
11. Pour cooked rice into serving bowls and top with meat and vegetables.

Serves 8

large gatherings. Along the coasts and rivers, people eat fish. A popular way of preparing fish is to cook it in coconut milk.

Jollof rice is a traditional western African dish made with onions, peppers, tomatoes, and pork or chicken. Check rice combines rice and okra. *Foo-foo* and *dumboy* are cassava dishes made with palm butter. Country chop is a dish of meats, fish, and vegetable greens, fried in palm oil. Rice bread is made by mixing rice and mashed bananas. Favorite desserts in Liberia include sweet potato pie, coconut pie, and pumpkin pie.

Adults enjoy ginger beer, made by combining powdered ginger, peeled pineapple, water, yeast, and molasses. Liberians also drink palm wine and coffee. They chew kola nuts for wakefulness and energy.

THE ECONOMY

Through much of its history, Liberia relied on trade in agricultural products, especially rubber and timber, to earn money. But the government ran up large budget deficits by spending more money than it brought in through trade and taxes. To make up the shortage, Liberia borrowed heavily from foreign countries. Paying back the loans emptied the government treasury, making it difficult for Liberia to develop its economy and attract new foreign investors.

In the years after World War II, Liberia's economy improved. Iron ore was discovered in the Nimba Mountains. The nation's iron, timber, and rubber businesses all thrived. With its strong economy, the country was able to build roads, schools, hospitals, and hydroelectric plants.

But the civil war that began in 1989 ravaged the Liberian economy. Fighting damaged roads, bridges, factories, and port facilities. Thousands of business leaders, teachers, doctors, and government workers, as well as ordinary laborers, left the country. Exports of iron ore, timber, rubber, and other products stopped. Liberia's gross domestic product (GDP, the value of goods and services produced in the country in one year) fell dramatically. People suffered from unemployment and poverty.

After the war, in 2004, the economy improved and the GDP grew. Exports resumed. Nevertheless, four out of every five Liberians still live below the official poverty line. The typical worker makes only about $25 a month—an extremely low wage that cannot sustain even a single worker, much less a family. About 70 percent of the labor force has no regular employment. To survive, many Liberians keep private gardens to grow rice and vegetables. They also barter handmade goods in streets and marketplaces.

◉ Agriculture

About 70 percent of workers in Liberia are farmers, and agriculture contributes about 77 percent of the country's GDP. Most farms are small, owned by a single family. Farmers typically grow rice and cassava for

THE RICE SEASON

Liberia's most important crop is rice. The time for planting rice is in March, at the start of the rainy season. Traditionally, women use short-handled hoes to plant rice seedlings in long furrows. The furrows flood with rainwater, and the seedlings grow tall from the surface of the water. Families build fences of branches and vines to keep out animals that want to eat the growing rice. Children patrol the fields with slingshots and rocks to frighten away hungry rice-eating birds. In November, at the start of the dry season, the rice harvest begins.

food. They also grow cash crops such as coffee and sugarcane, which they sell to local merchants and export companies. Other crops include plantains, bananas, coconuts, pineapples, and mangoes. Many farmers also raise chickens, goats, and sheep.

The rubber business in Liberia began in 1926 with the arrival of the U.S.-based Firestone Tire and Rubber Company. The company planted immense stands of rubber trees around Harbel and hired workers to collect the thick white latex used to make tires and other rubber products. During World War II, Liberia was a vital source of rubber for the Allied war effort. After the war, more companies from the United States and Europe set up latex-collecting operations in Liberia. In addition, some individual farmers collected latex to

Rice matures in a rice field near Monrovia, Liberia. Most rice in Liberia is grown for personal consumption.

An aging sign welcomes visitors to the **Firestone Rubber Plantation** near Harbel, Liberia. The world's largest latex farm has recently come under fire for unfair labor practices and conditions.

sell to rubber-processing factories. The rubber industry is still a major employer and exporter in Liberia.

Liberia's tropical hardwood trees, including teak, walnut, and mahogany, make up one of the country's vital natural resources. Lumber companies cut the trees to make furniture, homes, and other products. Many foreign companies own tree plantations in Liberia. The largest is the Oriental Timber Corporation of Indonesia. Logging contributes about one-quarter of Liberia's GDP and makes up slightly more than half of the country's exports.

Logging played an important role in the civil war of the 1990s. Militias fighting that war seized large stands of timber in Liberia's interior. These groups gave valuable hardwoods to foreign governments in exchange for money or weapons. This illegal logging extensively damaged the country's forest resources. In response, the United Nations has attempted to ban this trade.

Liberia has a small fishing industry, which employs about ten thousand people. A fleet of trawlers nets shrimp in the Sherbro fishing grounds, off the nation's northeastern coast. Small groups and

Many Liberian farming families belong to organizations called *kuu*. Kuu are cooperatives—businesses in which members pool their resources to help one another. Members of kuu share seeds and tools and market their crops together.

individuals use nets and lines to catch sea bream and sole near the shore. Fishers also take freshwater fish from Liberia's rivers. Some Liberian farmers have built fish hatcheries and ponds for fish breeding and raising. With foreign investment and loans, Liberia may develop a fish exporting industry, since shrimp, tuna, and lobster abound in the coastal waters.

Liberia's palm-oil industry has survived the civil war. Factories process the fruits of the palm-oil tree into cooking oil, margarine, and other products. But clearing land for palm-oil tree plantations destroys natural rain forest. This has earned palm oil the nickname of "cruel oil."

⊙ Manufacturing and Mining

Less than 10 percent of Liberians work in manufacturing and industry, and the manufacturing sector comprises about 5 percent of Liberia's GDP. Many factories and processing plants are foreign owned. Some plants process the raw latex for rubber. Others fashion iron ore into pellets for steel manufacturing. Buchanan holds the largest iron ore processing facility in Africa. Monrovia has chemical factories and an oil refinery (which was put out of action during the civil war). The nation also has cement factories, breweries, sawmills, food-processing plants, and sugar-refining operations.

In the 1940s and 1950s, European and U.S. mining companies arrived to extract iron ore from the Nimba Mountains, and iron mining and export became important businesses for Liberia. Most iron ore shipments

Taxi drivers stop to buy gasoline from a black market trader. Gasoline and many other goods can be found only on the black (illegal) market in Liberia.

left the country through the port of Buchanan. The civil war damaged mining equipment and transportation networks, however, and shut down the iron ore industry. The industry has just begun to recover from the damage. In addition to iron ore, Liberia has small gold and barite deposits, as well as deposits of hematite, magnetite, bauxite, and manganese ore.

Liberia began mining diamonds in the 1950s. But the diamond trade has brought abuse and corruption to the highest levels of government. During the civil war, corrupt officials used armed gangs to seize the diamonds. They also exchanged arms and soldiers from Liberia for stolen diamonds from rebel groups in Sierra Leone. Officials stashed these diamonds in private vaults or traded them on the international black (illegal) market for cash, weapons, or illegal drugs.

Liberia has no natural sources of crude oil, although oil deposits might exist offshore. As a result, Liberia must import refined gasoline.

Liberia does not produce its own oil, but refineries like this one process oil, turning it into gasoline and other fuels. Liberia's civil war crippled the nation's oil refineries, and many are still shut down.

Power generators at the **Mount Coffee Dam** were damaged during the Liberian civil war. Liberians rely on personal generators and batteries for electrical power.

The Mount Coffee Dam on the Saint Paul River was disabled during the civil war and still needs reconstruction. Thus the nation has no functioning electrical systems—even in the capital of Monrovia. Homeowners and businesses must use batteries and private generators to operate lights and appliances.

Service

The service sector includes banking, insurance, sales, tourism, and other businesses that provide services rather than goods or raw materials. About 22 percent of Liberia's workforce is employed in the service sector. Ship registration is one profitable service business for Liberia. The nation makes money by allowing foreign cargo ships and oil tankers to register as Liberian instead of registering with their home countries. By registering under the Liberian "flag of convenience," shipping companies pay less money than they would pay if registering at home. About two thousand foreign ships, including one-third of the world's oil-tanker fleet, are registered under the Liberian flag.

The recent civil war devastated many service businesses, especially the tourism business. During the fighting, many foreign countries issued warnings to their citizens, telling them not to travel to Liberia. Many hotels shut down for lack of running water, electricity, and other essentials. Tourism and other service industries have not yet recovered from the destruction.

Liberia's national flag flies on the masts of freighters, container ships, and passenger ships all over the world. About 35 percent of all oil tankers in the world are registered in Liberia. The ship-registry business brings in more than $13 million to Liberia every year.

◉ Transportation

Liberia's principal airport is the Roberts International Airport, 37 miles (59 km) from Monrovia in Margibi County. Airlines run flights between Roberts and the Ivory Coast, Guinea, Sierra Leone, and Ghana. There are no flights to Europe or North America, however. In recent years, warfare frequently shut down the airport, so Liberians had to travel by land or sea instead of air. Liberia's principal means of moving goods out of the country is cargo shipping.

Paved roads run from Monrovia to Buchanan and from Monrovia to the iron ore operations in Nimba County. A paved road network, built by the Firestone Company, also runs around the rubber operations in Harbel. In the rest of the country, people and vehicles move on narrow unpaved roads that suffer from a lack of maintenance and repairs.

Unpaved roads are common in Liberia. Only a few road networks are paved.

In heavy rains, roads often flood and wash out completely, preventing all vehicular travel. In all, Liberia has 6,586 miles (10,600 km) of roads, but only 408 miles (657 km) of them are paved.

Before the civil war, three railroads operated in Liberia. The railroads were used to ship iron ore, not to carry passengers. The civil war put the entire rail system out of action. The government has since dismantled the railroads and sold many of the rails as iron scrap to raise money.

The Future

An uneasy truce has ended the civil war that brought death and destruction to Liberia during the 1990s. The effects of the civil war—death and injury, damaged homes and schools, poor sanitation and health facilities, devastated families, and a ruined economy—still prevail. By some estimates, about 200,000 Liberians died. Another effect of the war was the drain of skilled workers, teachers, doctors, and business leaders who left to avoid the fighting. This exodus of talented Liberians has stymied the nation's effort to return to a peaceful existence.

When the warring factions ended their fighting in 2003, the United Nations sent peacekeeping forces to try to maintain the truce. An important part of this effort is the United Nations Mission in Liberia (UNMIL), which is attempting to disarm combatants and bring them back to civilian society. But the various rival factions within Liberia have kept their weapons and still operate armed camps. They remain ready and willing to return to war should the truce fail.

A variety of nonprofit groups are working in Liberia to rebuild the country. Africare, an international aid agency, is repairing hospitals and health clinics damaged during the war. In 2003 the Better Future Foundation began helping Liberian orphans and other children find needed food, shelter, and schooling. It also set a goal of achieving full literacy for Liberian adults as well as children.

In addition to these efforts, Liberia must hope for a return of

NEW PHONES

In 2004 Liberia set up its first cell phone network. The phones work in Monrovia, Harbel, Kabkata, Buchanan, and Robertsport. They represent the first reliable communication system for ordinary Liberians since the start of the civil war. Because the nation's landline system often does not work, thousands of Liberians have bought cell phones to communicate. The phones contain "smart cards." They have small computer chips that store information, such as phone numbers, text messages, and the user's name.

A U.S. aid team inspects a pier at **Monrovia harbor, Liberia,** for future rebuilding. The port city's docks were damaged during the civil war and must be fixed before the nation can again trade goods on world markets.

professionals and laborers who fled during the civil war, as well as new foreign investors and businesses. Foreign companies generally have the know-how and technicians needed to build modern roads, ports, and railroads. But these companies need political stability and safety for their workers to set up operations. If Liberia can manage a peaceful change to a newly elected president and legislature, then perhaps it can begin the journey of rebuilding its society and economy.

Visit www.vgsbooks.com for links to websites with additional information about Liberia's economy, economic recovery, growth, and outlook, as well as the country's future.

Timeline

1200s Settlers move to Liberia from the empires of Mali and Ghana to the north and east.

1461 The Portuguese navigator Pedro de Sintra explores the shores of western Africa.

1500s Mandingo traders arrive in Liberia.

1600s In search of valuable spices, slaves, and ivory, Dutch, English, and French traders arrive at the Grain Coast.

1816 Robert Finley founds the American Colonization Society (ACS) to settle freed slaves in Africa.

1818 ACS members and U.S. officials explore the Grain Coast for future settlement sites.

1820 The first ACS ship, the *Elizabeth*, arrives off the coast of Sierra Leone.

1822 Jehudi Ashmun draws up a peace treaty between settlers and indigenous people of the Grain Coast.

1824 The ACS names the new colony Liberia and renames its capital city Monrovia (the city was called Christopolis for two years), after President James Monroe.

1825-1826 Jehudi Ashmun negotiates with King Peter, an indigenous chief, who agrees to sell land to American settlers in return for gunpowder and other goods.

1839 The ACS appoints Thomas Buchanan as the first governor of Liberia.

1841 Joseph Jenkins Roberts becomes the first black governor of Liberia.

1847 Liberians adopt a declaration of independence and elect Joseph Jenkins Roberts as president.

1857 The settlement known as Maryland County joins Liberia.

1862 The United States formally recognizes Liberia as an independent nation.

1863 Liberia College is founded in Monrovia.

1871 The Liberian government negotiates a $500,000 loan from Great Britain. President Edward Roye is charged with stealing the money and is overthrown in a coup.

1893 The Grebo people stage an uprising and a massacre in Harper.

1912 European nations and the United States extend a new loan Liberia to help solve the country's financial crisis.

1914 World War I begins in Europe.

1917 Liberia joins the nations fighting Germany and its allies.

1926   The Firestone Tire and Rubber Company leases a 1 million-
        acre (404,678-hectare) rubber plantation in Liberia.

1939   World War II begins in Europe.

1944   William V. S. Tubman becomes Liberia's president. Liberia joins the Allies
        fighting in World War II.

1945   Liberian women and indigenous people gain the right to vote. Liberia joins the
        United Nations.

1971   William R. Tolbert takes office as president.

1980   Samuel Doe overthrows the Tolbert government in a violent coup. Doe's followers
        assassinate Tolbert and execute thirteen cabinet ministers.

1986   Liberia draws up a new constitution.

1989   A rebel group, the National Patriotic Front of Liberia, invades Liberia. Civil war begins.

1990   A rebel faction under Prince Johnson captures and kills Samuel Doe.

1993   The United Nations arranges a truce among the factions fighting in Liberia. The truce
        does not hold.

1996   The factions in Liberia sign the Abuja II Accord, which helps end the civil war.

1996   Ruth Perry is elected head of the Council of State.

1997   Charles Taylor is elected president after eight years of civil war. Ethnic conflict continues,
        heavily damaging Monrovia.

2003   Charles Taylor flees Liberia for refuge in Nigeria. Gyude Bryant is named interim president
        and takes office. Elections are scheduled for 2005.

2005   Ellen Johnson-Sirleaf claims victory over opponent George Manneh Weah during a
        highly contested presidential runoff. She promises to unite and rebuild the country
        despite Weah's accusations that the election was rigged. The election is Liberia's
        first free election in fourteen years of civil war and Johnson-Sirleaf becomes
        Africa's first democratically elected woman president.

COUNTRY NAME Republic of Liberia

AREA 43,000 square miles (111,370 sq. km)

MAIN LANDFORMS Bong Range, Cape Mesurado, Cape Palmas, Mano Hills, Nimba Mountains, Putu Range, Wologizi Mountains

HIGHEST POINT Mount Wutivi, 4,613 feet (1,406 m) above sea level

MAJOR RIVERS Cavalla, Cestos, Grand Cess, Lofa, Mano, Saint John, Saint Paul

ANIMALS antelopes, crocodiles, elephants, flamingos, honey badgers, hornbills, leopards, mongooses, monkeys, parrots, pygmy hippopotamuses, water buffalo, woodpeckers

CAPITAL CITY Monrovia

OTHER MAJOR CITIES Buchanan, Harbel, Robertsport

OFFICIAL LANGUAGE English

MONETARY UNITS Liberian dollar. 1 dollar = 100 cents

LIBERIAN CURRENCY

Liberia began minting coins during the 1850s. The coins had the same denominations as U.S. coins: pennies, nickels, dimes, quarters, and dollars. Liberians used these coins until the 1980s, when the Doe government began printing Liberian dollar bills (called liberties), modeled after U.S. currency.

During the civil war in the early 1990s, a rebel faction looted the Central Bank of Liberia, stealing vast amounts of currency. Because so much money was stolen, the government declared Liberian dollar notes illegal. The government issued new notes, but merchants in rebel-held areas did not accept the notes.

In 1997, under newly elected President Charles Taylor, the Liberian treasury designed a new series of notes, in denominations of L$5, L$10, L$20, L$50, and L$100. Liberians call the Taylor-era dollars JJs, after the portrait of President J. J. Roberts that appears on the Liberian five-dollar bill.

A committee of seven women, all members of Americo-Liberian families and headed by Susanna Waring-Lewis, designed the Liberian flag in the mid-1800s. Adopted in 1847, the Liberian flag carries six red and five white horizontal stripes. The eleven stripes stand for the eleven signers of Liberia's declaration of independence. The upper left corner of the flag is a field of blue with a single five-pointed white star, celebrating Liberia's status as the first independent republic on the African continent. Blue represents liberty and justice, while white represents purity, and red symbolizes courage and valor.

Flag

Liberia's national anthem is "All Hail, Liberia, Hail!" Daniel Bashiel Warner, the third president of Liberia, wrote the words. Olmstead Luca wrote the music. Liberia officially adopted the anthem when it declared its independence in 1847. These are the words to the first verse:

National Anthem

All Hail, Liberia, Hail!
All hail, Liberia, hail!
All hail, Liberia, hail!
This glorious land of liberty
Shall long be ours.
Though new her name,
Green be her fame,
And mighty be her powers,
And mighty be her powers.
In joy and gladness
With our hearts united,
We'll shout the freedom
Of a race benighted,
Long live Liberia, happy land!

 Visit www.vgsbooks.com for a link to the complete lyrics of Liberia's national anthem and to access a sound clip of it.

JEHUDI ASHMUN (1794–1828) Born in Champlain, New York, Ashmun was a minister and missionary. An agent of the American Colonization Society, he arrived in Liberia in 1822 to help the struggling settlement. Ashmun helped the settlers beat back attacks by indigenous people and negotiate for land. He also helped set up the government of the future nation. He left Liberia in 1828, sailed to Boston, and soon thereafter died of an illness contracted in Africa.

EDWARD BLYDEN (1832–1912) Born in Saint Thomas in the Virgin Islands, Blyden emigrated from there to Liberia in 1850. He was committed to pan-Africanism, the movement to unify all African nations and to end European control. He founded several western African newspapers and wrote books examining African culture and history, including *A Voice from Bleeding Africa; Liberia's Offering;* and *Christianity, Islam, and the Negro Race.*

PAUL CUFFEE (1759–1817) Born near New Bedford, Massachusetts, Cuffee was a wealthy African American merchant who played an important role in the African American colonization movement. In 1816 Cuffee sailed to Sierra Leone with forty former slaves as passengers. After helping his passengers settle in Africa, Cuffee planned to return to the United States with a cargo of ivory and other valuable goods, but he died before leaving Africa. Cuffee's voyage inspired members of the American Colonization Society to plan the settlement of freed slaves along the coast of western Africa.

ROLAND DEMPSTER (1910–1965) Born in Tosoh, Liberia, Dempster attended a missionary school in his village. In 1948 he became editor of a biweekly newspaper, the *Liberian Age.* That same year, he became an English and writing professor at the University of Liberia, a post he held until 1960. In his poetry, articles, and stories, Dempster praised the government of President Tubman and celebrated the progress Liberia was making in the years after World War II.

MIATTA FANBULLEH (b. 1950) A vocalist and music producer born in Monrovia, Fanbulleh made her professional debut at the Apollo Theater in New York. She has performed with African and American jazz artists, including Donald Byrd and Hugh Masekela. Fanbulleh wrote "Amo Sake Sa" and "Kokolioko," both hit songs throughout western Africa.

BAI T. MOORE (b. 1916) A member of the Gola people, Moore was born in Vai, Liberia. His parents immigrated to the United States in the 1920s, and he attended schools in Richmond, Virginia, before returning to his native land. After being severely injured in a plane crash in 1954, he began writing poetry, collecting his works in *Ebony Dust.* In 1968 he published *Murder in the Cassava Patch,* the Liberian novel best known to the outside world.

HAWA MOORE (b. 1955) Born in Negban, a member of the Vai people, Moore was the granddaughter of an indigenous king. She began writing music at the age of five and performed solo and in group ensembles. She toured with South African singer Miriam Makeba in the 1970s and made three popular records in Liberia during the 1980s. She escaped the Liberian civil war in 1991 and moved to the United States, where she founded the group Akpandayah to promote western African music and dance.

RUTH SANDO PERRY (b. 1939) Born in Dia, Liberia, Ruth Perry attended Saint Theresa Convent High School and the University of Liberia, where she obtained a teaching degree. She entered business and banking and served as a supervisor of the Chase Manhattan Bank of Liberia. Getting involved in politics, she won election as a senator from Grand Cape Mount County. In 1996, after the overthrow of Samuel K. Doe, she was elected unanimously as the chairperson of the Council of State, becoming the first female head of state in Africa. The next year, Charles Taylor was elected president, replacing Perry as head of state.

JOSEPH JENKINS ROBERTS (1809–1876) Roberts was born a free African American in Norfolk, Virginia. He arrived in Africa as a young settler in 1829. He became high sheriff of Liberia in 1833 and began serving as vice governor in 1838. Roberts became Liberia's first black governor in 1841 on the death of Thomas Buchanan. He then helped establish the Republic of Liberia in 1847 and became the republic's first president.

ELLEN JOHNSON-SIRLEAF (b. 1938) Born in Monrovia, Ellen Johnson-Sirleaf overcame poverty, receiving a degree from Harvard University and holding positions in the Liberian government and the World Bank. An activist, Johnson spoke out against injustices and violence committed by the Liberian government. She went into exile in 1985, returning to Liberia in 1997 and entering politics. In 2005 Johnson-Sirleaf ran for president in Liberia's first free democratic election in fourteen years of civil war. In November 2005, she is named Liberia's president-elect, Africa's first democratically elected woman head of state.

WILLIAM V. S. TUBMAN (1895–1971) Born in Harper, Liberia, William Tubman was a leader of the True Whig Party and served as president of Liberia from 1944 until his death in 1971. Tubman oversaw Liberia's post–World War II years, the building of new port facilities and manufacturing businesses, and Liberian participation in the United Nations. Tubman aligned Liberia with the United States during the Cold War between the United States and Communist governments and made Liberia into an outpost of pro-U.S. foreign policy in Africa.

GEORGE WEAH (b. 1966) Born in Monrovia, George Weah is a soccer forward who played for several teams in Liberia. He then moved to Europe, where he played for teams in Monaco, Great Britain, France, and Italy. In 2005 Weah returned to Liberia to run for president.

Liberia has an interesting history and a landscape of natural beauty. While these qualities give the country many sights to visit in times of peace, instability still leaves Liberia a risky destination for tourists. Anyone considering a trip to Liberia should check with the U.S. State Department (see the website at http://travel.state.gov/travel_ warnings.html) and with embassies in Liberia for travel safety status.

FIRESTONE RUBBER PLANTATION The largest rubber plantation in the world, the Firestone plantation is about 30 miles (48 km) east of Monrovia around the town of Harbel. Visitors can take guided tours of the plantation and learn how rubber is collected and processed.

FORT NORRIS This old fort on Ducor Hill overlooks Monrovia and Cape Mesurado. The fort is the site of the famous Matilda Newport Cannon, fired by an early settler named Matilda Newport to fend off an attack. The cannon stands in the middle of a small monument. The fort also holds a statue of J. J. Roberts, the first president of Liberia.

KENDEJA CULTURAL CENTER The Liberian government dedicated this building to the ethnic groups and cultures of Monrovia. A museum here shows how the different ethnic groups of Liberia built their homes. Visitors can watch mask makers exhibit their skill in carving, shaping, and decorating wooden masks. They can also listen to folk music and see dance troupes perform.

LAKE PISO The country's largest lake lies about 50 miles (80 km) northwest of Monrovia. Fishing boats, canoes, and water-skiers glide across the lake's surface, while swimmers can frolic in the water. The lake is the site of Massatin Island, named for Massa, a woman who lived and farmed alone on the island in the fifteenth century.

MONROVIA The national capital is the site of important government buildings, monuments, nineteenth-century churches, street markets, and restaurants known as cookshops. In the evening, Monrovians gather on Gurley Street, the city's entertainment center, where they enjoy live-music clubs or dancing in one of the street's many discos.

PROVIDENCE ISLAND The island was the site of the landing of the first settlers from the United States. Settlers and indigenous people also signed a treaty here beneath a kapok tree. The tree survived the many battles of the civil war and still stands. The island also holds museums of history and indigenous arts.

SAPO NATIONAL RIVER this 505-square-mile (1,308 sq. km) game reserve along the Sinoe River protects a wide variety of threatened wildlife, including pygmy hippopotamuses, elephants, monkeys, antelopes, leopards, and crocodiles. The park contains only a few rough trails, and parts of it have never been explored.

Americo-Liberian: a descendant of free African Americans who came to live in Liberia in the nineteenth century

animist: a person who follows a religion honoring spirits of the sky, forest, natural world, and ancestors

black market: trade in illegal goods such as weapons and drugs

colonize: to send soldiers, settlers, and government officials to take possession of a new land

coup: overthrow and takeover of a government, often by violent means

hydroelectricity: electrical power produced by damming a river and then harnessing the energy of the moving water

lagoon: a small coastal pool formed at the mouth of a river or by the movement of ocean tides

latex: the thick, white sap of rubber trees; used to make rubber

militia: an informal or citizen army

missionary: a person who tries to convert people to his or her religion

pidgin: a simplified form of speech that allows people who speak different languages to communicate. In Liberia people use a pidgin language that mixes English with African words and phrases.

refugee: a person who flees to a foreign country to escape danger or persecution

subsistence farming: growing just enough food to feed one's own family

tropical rain forest: a forest that grows in a region with high annual rainfall

Glossary

Selected Bibliography

CIA World Factbook: Liberia. 2005.
http://www.cia.gov/cia/publications/factbook/geos/li.html **(October 2005).**
This site is a useful resource, with up-to-date statistics on Liberian geography, population, economy, communications, transportation, the military, and health, as well as maps and a description of the Liberian government.

Clegg, Claude A. *The Price of Liberty: African Americans and the Making of Liberia*. Chapel Hill: University of North Carolina Press, 2004.
This book explores the origins and experiences of African Americans who undertook the hazardous voyage to and settlement of Liberia.

Corder, Henry S., ed. *New Voices from Liberia*. Newark: University of Delaware Press, 1979.
This collection contains writings from Liberian authors.

Daniels, Antony. *Monrovia Mon Amour: A Visit to Liberia*. London: John Murray, 1993.
The author describes a visit to the war-ravaged capital of Monrovia and gives an account of the politics of the civil war.

Ellis, Stephan. *The Mask of Anarchy: The Destruction of Liberia and the Religious Dimension of a Civil War*. New York: New York University Press, 2001.
This book provides a history of the civil war in Liberia, focusing on the use of ritual and costume, as well as the religious aspects of war.

Greene, Graham. *Journey without Maps*. New York: Penguin, 1992.
The author describes a long and hard journey by foot through the back country of Liberia and his encounter with Liberian village chiefs and government officials.

Huffman, Alan. *Mississippi in Africa: The Saga of the Slaves of Prospect Hill Plantation and Their Legacy in Liberia Today*. New York: Gotham Books, 2004.
The author traces the history of a Mississippi plantation owner who releases his slaves to Africa and how these people became the ruling class of Liberia.

Kulah, Arthur F. *Liberia Will Rise Again: Reflections on the Liberian Civil Crisis*. Nashville: Abingdon, 1999.
A Methodist bishop describes the Liberian civil war firsthand and his hope for a peaceful and unified country.

Pham, John-Peter. *Liberia: Portrait of a Failed State*. New York: Reed Press, 2004.
This book provides a general history of Liberia, from its first settlement by freed slaves from the United States to the presidency of Charles Taylor.

Powers, William. *Blue Clay People: Seasons on Africa's Fragile Edge*. New York: Bloomsbury USA, 2005.
An aid worker recounts his experiences in Liberia, his travel through the country's poor and war-torn countryside, and the many problems he faced while trying to help Liberians.

Reef, Catherine. *This Our Dark Country: The American Settlers of Liberia.* **New York: Clarion, 2002.**
Reef's book is a photo essay containing letters, diary entries, and other primary documents that explain the early settlement of Liberia by African Americans.

Stryker, Richard Lane. *Forged from Chaos: Stories and Reflections from Liberia at War.* **Bloomington, IN: 1st Books Library, 2003.**
This book offers a harrowing account of the civil war in Liberia.

Williams, Gabriel I. H. *Liberia: The Heart of Darkness.* **Victoria, BC: Trafford, 2002.**
A Liberian newspaper editor describes the civil war begun by Charles Taylor's National Patriotic Front of Liberia and the fighting that took place before Williams fled for his own safety in 1993.

African-American Mosaic: Colonization
http://lcweb.loc.gov/exhibits/african/afam002.html
This page is dedicated to the history of the Back-to-Africa colonization movement, with an essay, photographs, documents, and a historical map of Liberia.

African Studies Page: Liberia
http://www.sas.upenn.edu/African_Studies/Country_Specific/Liberia.html
This is a page of useful links to Liberia-related websites covering history, languages, art, and current events.

All about Liberia
http://www.pbs.org/wgbh/globalconnections/liberia/essays/history/index.html
This website is run by and for Liberians in Liberia. It offers news and opinion articles concentrating on settlement of the civil conflict.

Carey, Robert D., and John Harvey Furbay. *Freedom Ships: The Spectacular Epic of African Americans Who Dared to Find Their Freedom Long before Emancipation.* Topeka, KS: Af-Am Links Press, 1999.
This historical novel describes the life of freed U.S. slaves who settled the Grain Coast of western Africa in 1820.

Dendel, Esther Warner. *You Cannot Unsneeze a Sneeze and Other Tales from Liberia.* Boulder: University Press of Colorado, 1995.
The author presents forty short Liberian folktales in pidgin English.

Global Connections: Liberia
http://www.pbs.org/wgbh/globalconnections/liberia/
This site is based on the documentary film *America's Stepchild: Liberia.* The site includes essays about the history of Liberia, a timeline of important events, and links.

Huffman, Alan. *Mississippi in Africa: The Saga of the Slaves of Prospect Hill Plantation and Their Legacy in Liberia Today.* New York: Gotham, 2004.
This book describes how Isaac Ross, a Mississippi plantation owner, arranged in his will to free two hundred slaves and move them to Liberia. It also details how the freed slaves rebuilt plantation society in the new Liberian republic.

Levy, Patricia. *Liberia.* Tarrytown, NY: Marshall Cavendish, 1998.
The author describes the geography, history, government, economy, lifestyle, culture, religion, language, arts, and food of Liberia in this young adult library book.

Liberian Connection
http://www.Liberian-Connection.com/
This website offers news and cultural events concerning Liberia, with chat rooms, discussion forums, a radio connection, photographs, sports news, and links to other Liberian sites on the Internet.

Further Reading and Websites

Moses, Wilson Jeremiah, ed. *Liberian Dreams: Back-to-Africa Narratives from the 1850s.* University Park: Pennsylvania State University Press, 1998.
This collection presents the writings of nineteenth-century African Americans who settled in the new Republic of Liberia.

Reef, Catherine. *This Our Dark Country: The American Settlers of Liberia.* New York: Clarion, 2002.
This history of Liberia for young readers is illustrated with prints and photographs. In telling the story, the author quotes from primary sources such as diaries, letters, and speeches.

Rosario, Paul. *Liberia.* Milwaukee: Gareth Stevens, 2003.
This short book for young readers examines the geography, history, and culture of Liberia.

vgsbooks.com
http://www.vgsbooks.com
Visit vgsbooks.com, the homepage of the Visual Geography Series®. You can get linked to all sorts of useful on-line information, including geographical, historical, demographic, cultural, and economic websites. The vgsbooks.com site is a great resource for late-breaking news and statistics.

Zemser, Amy Bronwen. *Beyond the Mango Tree.* New York: HarperCollins, 2000.
This novel describes the experiences of a young white girl who lives in modern Liberia and who encounters a fascinating and frightening world entirely different from her own.

Captions for photos appearing on cover and chapter openers:

Cover: The capital city of Monrovia sits along the Atlantic coast in northwestern Liberia. For many decades the city was a thriving port of trade.

pp. 4–5 The western coast of Liberia has sandy beaches, tropical rain forest, and marshy wetlands.

pp. 8–9 A vine-woven bridge spans a river in Liberia's rain forest. Clear-cut logging and destruction from years of civil war have threatened the country's once flourishing rain forests.

pp. 18–19 In this painting from the late 1400s or early 1500s, ships sail out of the harbor at Lisbon, Portugal, some destined for exploration of new lands. The Portuguese explored and mapped the coastline of Liberia in the fifteenth century.

pp. 36–37 People go about their day in downtown Monrovia, Liberia, in the early 2000s. Fourteen years of civil war have wracked the capital city.

pp. 44–45 A Kpelle woman weaves a palm-fiber bag in her Liberian village.

pp. 56–57 A workers' settlement stands in a clearing of rubber tree forest on the Firestone Tire and Rubber Plantation near Harbel, Liberia. Firestone/Bridgestone, the corporate owner of the plantation, is slowly pulling out of Liberia, selling off its older, less productive stands of trees to local growers. Liberia produces much of the world's natural latex used in rubber production.

Photo Acknowledgments

The images in this book are used with the permission of: © Phil Porter, pp. 4–5, 8–9, 56–57; XNR Productions, pp. 6, 12; © Hutchison/Dirk R. Frans, pp. 10, 14, 39, 47, 63; © Martin Harvey/CORBIS, p. 11; © Heldur Netocny/Panos Pictures, pp. 16–17, 36–37; © North Wind Picture Archives, pp. 18–19; Library of Congress, pp. 20 (LC-DIG-ppmsca-05933), 46 (LC-USZ6-1944); © CORBIS, p. 25; © Mary Evans Picture Library/The Image Works, p. 27; © Keystone/Hulton Archive/Getty Images, p. 28; © AFP/Getty Images, p. 29; © Francois Rojon/AFP/Getty Images, p. 31; © Joel Robine/AFP/Getty Images, p. 32; © Scott Peterson/Liaison Agency/Getty Images, p. 33; © Taleb Ahmed/Panapress/Getty Images, p. 34; © Liba Taylor/Panos Pictures, pp. 40, 54; © Hutchison/Stephen Pera, p. 41; © Giacomo Pirozzi/Panos Pictures, p. 42; © Jacques Jangoux/Photo Researchers, Inc., pp. 44–45; © STR/AFP/Getty Images, p. 48; © SuperStock, Inc./SuperStock, p. 49; © Malcolm Linton/Liaison Agency/Getty Images, p. 50; © Hutchison/Liba Taylor, p. 51; © Issouf Sanogo/AFP/Getty Images, p. 53; © Eric Miller/Panos Pictures, pp. 58, 59; © Pius Utomi Ekpei/AFP/Getty Images, p. 60; © J. Hartley/Panos Pictures, p. 61; © Hutchison/John Gaisford, p. 62; © Patrick Robert/CORBIS, p. 65; Audrius Tomonis—www.banknotes.com, p. 68; Laura Westlund, p. 69.

Front Cover: © Heldur Netocny/Panos Pictures. Back Cover: NASA.